Canto is a paperback imprint which offers a broad range of titles, both classic and more recent, representing some of the best and most enjoyable of Cambridge publishing.

C. P. SNOW

THE TWO CULTURES

with Introduction by

STEFAN COLLINI

CAMBRIDGE
UNIVERSITY PRESS

PUBLISHED BY THE PRESS SYNDICATE OF THE UNIVERSITY OF CAMBRIDGE
The Pitt Building, Trumpington Street, Cambridge, United Kingdom

CAMBRIDGE UNIVERSITY PRESS
The Edinburgh Building, Cambridge CB2 2RU, UK
40 West 20th Street, New York, NY 10011–4211, USA
477 Williamstown Road, Port Melbourne, VIC 3207, Australia
Ruiz de Alarcón 13, 28014 Madrid, Spain
Dock House, The Waterfront, Cape Town 8001, South Africa

http://www.cambridge.org

Part 1 first published 1959
Reprinted 1959 (three times), 1960 (three times), 1961 (twice), 1962 (twice)
Part II added 1964
Reprinted 1965
First paperback edition 1969
Reprinted 1972, 1974, 1976, 1978, 1979, 1980, 1981, 1982, 1983, 1984, 1986 (twice),
1987, 1988, 1991, 1992
Canto edition 1993
Reprinted 1998, 2000, 2001, 2002, 2003, 2005, 2006

Printed in Great Britain by Biddles Limited, Guildford & King's Lynn

ISBN 0 521 06520 8 hardback
ISBN 0 521 45730 0 paperback

Cover illustration: detail from *Arcone con le Sibille,* Raffaello.
S. Maria della Pace, Rome/Bridgeman Art Library.

GE

CONTENTS

INTRODUCTION

At a few minutes past five o'clock in the afternoon of 7 May 1959, a bulky, shambling figure approached the lectern at the western end of the Senate House in Cambridge. In the body of the ornately plastered neo-classical building sat a large gathering of dons and students, together with a number of distinguished guests, who had assembled for one of Cambridge's show-piece public occasions, the annual Rede lecture. The figure who was about to address them was C.P. Snow (then more formally styled Sir Charles, soon to be Lord Snow, but known throughout the world by his initials). Snow had been a research scientist; he had high-level administrative experience in the Civil Service and in private industry; he was a successful novelist and prominent reviewer; and he had now achieved the indefinable status of a 'public figure', licensed to announce his opinions on all manner of topics. By the time he sat down over an hour later, Snow had done at least three things: he had launched a phrase, perhaps even a concept, on an unstoppably successful inter-national career; he had formulated a question (or, as it turned out, several questions) which any reflective observer of modern societies needs to address; and he had started a controversy which was to be remarkable for its scope, its duration, and, at least at times, its intensity.

The title of Snow's lecture was 'The Two Cultures and the Scientific Revolution'. The 'two cultures' he identified were those of 'the literary intellectuals' (as he called them) and of the natural scientists, between whom he claimed to find a profound mutual suspicion and incomprehension, which in turn had damaging consequences for the prospects of applying technology to the alleviation of the world's problems. But in broaching this topic to his Cambridge audience, Snow was thrusting into the spotlight of public discussion themes which found an echo across the globe and which have continued to preoccupy and provoke. For in effect Snow was doing more than asking what the relation should be between the two cultures he believed he had identified, and doing more even than asking how the curricula of schools and universities should be arranged to give people an adequate education in both branches of knowledge. Beyond those pressing and consequential questions, he was asking what Britain's place was to be among the leading countries of the world; he was asking how (not whether but how) the rich countries should help the poor; he was asking how the planet was to be fed and what hopes for mankind the future held. Whatever reservations we may now have about the adequacy of Snow's original formulations, it is impossible to feel that the confusing and distressing period of history that divides us from the apparently more confident world of 1959 has rendered these questions any less urgent or any more tractable.

The large topics raised by Snow are not the exclusive property of any one discipline; indeed, they legitimately claim the attention of any educated citizen, and should not be confined to a set of academic pigeon-holes. Obviously, they are continuous with the *kinds* of topic which are habitually considered by philosophers, historians, and sociologists; how far they should also be considered part of the primary professional activity of physicists, chemists, and biologists has precisely been one of the matters at stake in the subsequent debate. For these reasons, it ought to be clear that to address the origins and significance of the idea of the 'two cultures' from the perspective of the cultural historian is not to assert some sort of superiority of the humanities over the sciences, still less is it any slighting of the immense importance of science or a high-handed dismissal of the perspective of the working scientist. However, Snow and his ideas are beginning to encounter a fate which is common among episodes of recent intellectual history: they fall into a murky limbo, no longer accurately recalled as part of living contemporary culture but not yet beginning to benefit from patient historical reconstruction. Before trying to identify what force and relevance Snow's questions still possess, therefore, it may be helpful to accelerate his release from this limbo by considering his work and its impact historically. But, first, a brief glance at the pre-history of this debate may help to set the topic in a longer perspective.

The 'two cultures' in historical perspective

As a cultural anxiety, concern about the divide between the 'two cultures' essentially dates from the nineteenth century, and the modern form of this anxiety would have been barely intelligible in earlier periods. Certainly, there have been, from the Greek dawn of Western thought onwards, distinct domains of human knowledge, and at different times reflective minds have pondered the dangers involved when one branch or 'discipline' of enquiry comes to be either threateningly dominant or inaccessibly recondite. But throughout the Middle Ages and Renaissance the interpretation of nature was generally regarded as but one element in the all-embracing enterprise of 'philosophy'. Only in the seventeenth century, in the course of what historians were much later to dub 'the scientific revolution', did achievements in the study of the natural world come to be widely regarded as setting new standards for what could count as genuine knowledge, and thereafter the methods employed by the 'natural philosophers' (as they were still termed) enjoyed a special cultural authority. The recurrence during the eighteenth-century Enlightenment of the aspiration to be 'the Newton of the moral sciences' testifies to the prestige not just of celestial mechanics, but of 'the experimental method' more generally. But that phrase also indicates that the study of human affairs could be seen as on a continuum with understanding the natural world, and the cultural map provided by the Enlightenment's great intellectual monument, *L'Encyclopédie*, did not represent human knowledge as structured around a division corresponding to the later divide between 'the sciences' and 'the humanities'.

It is from the Romantic period, at the end of the eighteenth and beginning of the nineteenth centuries, that one can date the beginning of an anxiety that some such fissure in types of knowledge might be opening up in a way which damaged both individual cultivation and social well-being. But even at this point, the threat was still not necessarily to be identified as an incapacity to communicate across a divide separating students of the human and of the natural worlds. It is true that William Blake, among others, memorably excoriated Newton and his legacy, but the Romantic champions of the imagination were as likely to contrast the fulness of creative or emotional energy released by poetry with the impoverished conception of human life underlying the 'dismal science' of political economy as to draw the line between the study of the human and the natural world. Insofar as a more general cultural worry was expressed, it was that calculation and measurement generally might be displacing cultivation and compassion, and of course in many quarters the over-riding issue was rather the presumed threat which secular knowledge of all kinds posed to religious belief and practical piety.[1]

Intellectual activity, including the meta-activity of reflection on the forms of knowledge, is, of course, shaped by different national traditions and anchored in a range of social practices. One can trace a specifically British genealogy for the 'two cultures' anxiety, arising out of a distinctive development of the social institutions within which education and research were carried on. This distinctiveness was reflected in the linguistic peculiarity by which the term 'science' came to be used in a narrowed sense to refer just to the 'physical' or 'natural' sciences. This appears to have become common in English only in the middle of the nineteenth century. The compilers of the *Oxford English Dictionary*, setting to work in the late-nineteenth century, recognised that this was a relatively recent development; the dictionary gives no example of this sense before the 1860s, and it is revealing that its first illustrative quotation implicitly points to the way English usage had started to diverge from other European languages: 'We shall . . . use the word "science" in the sense which Englishmen so commonly give to it; as expressing

[1] For a brief overview of this pre-history see Wolf Lepenies, *Between Literature and Science: The Rise of Sociology* ((1985) Eng. trans., Cambridge, 1988), 'Introduction'. The original German title, *Die Drei Kulturen*, makes the link to Snow's thesis explicit.

physical and experimental science, to the exclusion of theological and metaphysical.'[2] Similarly, the coinage 'scientist' and its restriction to those practising the natural sciences is no older than the 1830s and 1840s. Credit for securely establishing the term is usually given to the philosopher and historian of science William Whewell, who used it in his *The Philosophy of the Inductive Sciences* of 1840. But the term first appeared in an article of 1834 reporting on how the lack of a single term to describe 'students of the knowledge of the material world' had bothered meetings of the British Association for the Advancement of Science in the early 1830s, at one of which 'some ingenious gentleman proposed that, by analogy with *artist*, they might form *scientist*', though the same report records that 'this was not generally palatable'.[3] Its subsequent currency reflected the growth of a self-conscious sense of professional identity among those who studied the natural world, an essential social precondition for later concerns about the divide between rival 'cultures'.

But the key social activity which posed with a pressing urgency the problem of the relation of the increasingly separate 'sciences' to the rest of culture was, of course, education. This was true in all the major European states, as national systems of education were put into place in the course of the nineteenth century, but again it took an especially acute form in England

[2] The quotation is from W.G. Ward in *The Dublin Review* (1867); see *OED*, 'science', sense 5. The *Supplement* to the dictionary, published in 1987, simply says 'this is now the dominant sense in ordinary use'.

[3] [William Whewell], '*The Connection of the Sciences* by Mrs Somerville', *Quarterly Review*, 101 (1834), 59. For the suggestion that the 'ingenious gentleman' was Whewell himself, see Sydney Ross, 'Scientist: the Story of a Word', *Annals of Science*, 18 (1962), 65–85.

(Scotland retained a broader as well as more democratic pattern of education). For social at least as much as for intellectual reasons, a classical education at public school, followed by a sojourn at Oxford or Cambridge, remained the most prestigious educational route well into the twentieth century (though mathematics had long been held to be on a par with classics as a form of mental exercise). The teaching of science did gradually infiltrate these elite institutions – the establishment of a course in the natural sciences at Cambridge in 1850 was a significant landmark, and the endowment by the Duke of Devonshire in 1870 of the Cavendish Laboratory there was another. But in some quarters it continued to be stigmatised as a vocational and slightly grubby activity, not altogether suitable for the proper education of a gentleman. Indeed, at all levels science had to struggle to gain anything like parity in the curriculum, and the applied sciences in particular continued (and perhaps still continue) to be regarded as inferior activities in both the educational and industrial worlds.[4] By a nice irony, the canonical confrontation between the champions of scientific and literary education in the nineteenth century, which partly anticipated the debate between Snow and his chief adversary from the ranks of the literary critics, F.R. Leavis, also involved a Rede lecture at Cambridge.

In the late-nineteenth century, science had no more redoubtable and out-spoken champion than T.H. Huxley, a distinguished naturalist and comparative anatomist who had been Professor at the Royal School of Mines and who played a leading part in founding the

[4] Eric Ashby, *Technology and the Academics: An Essay on Technology and the Universities* (London, 1958), esp. chs. 2 and 3. Snow cites this work approvingly at p. 23 below.

scientific teaching institution which was to become Imperial College, London. Invited to give the address to mark the opening in 1880 of Mason College, an institution founded in Birmingham in the heart of industrial England explicitly to provide a scientific education for those intending to pursue careers in manufacturing and commerce, Huxley issued a challenge to the defenders of the traditional classical education. Science, he affirmed, formed part of culture and offered a rigorous mental training, as well as making an indispensable contribution to national well-being. In tones that were to become familiar in the subsequent century, he denounced the resistance to the claims of scientific education by the defenders of the traditional classical curriculum as, therefore, both unjustified and short-sighted.[5]

Huxley's lecture contained a friendly allusion to the way in which the defenders of classical education drew comfort from the writings of 'our chief apostle of culture', that is, of Matthew Arnold. By this date, Arnold was the leading man of letters in Victorian England, but his working life had been spent as an Inspector of Schools, so he was regarded as speaking with a double authority on questions of education. When he came to deliver the Rede lecture for 1882 in the same Senate House that was later to be the setting for Snow, Arnold proposed as his theme 'Literature and Science', and he explicitly took up the challenge of Huxley's address. His tactic was essentially to re-define terms until the sharp contrast that Huxley had drawn between a literary and a scientific education all but disappeared. He insisted that the category of 'literature'

[5] T.H. Huxley, 'Science and Culture' (1880), repr. in his *Science and Education: Essays* (London, 1893), pp. 134–59.

should embrace not mere *belles-lettres* but all great classics including Newton's *Principia* and Darwin's *The Origin of Species*. Similarly, he argued that Huxley was confining 'science' to the narrow English sense; the study of languages and of history could be part of systematic knowledge or *Wissenschaft*. Arnold thus made it easy for himself to conclude eirenically that literature and science were not so wholly dissimilar to one another, and that both deserved a place in a rounded education. But beneath this show of agreeableness, Arnold was in fact unyielding in resisting Huxley's attempted promotion of scientific and demotion of classical education. Above all, he insisted that a training in the natural sciences might produce a practically valuable specialist, but it could not turn out an 'educated' man: for this, literature, especially the literatures of antiquity, remained indispensable.[6]

This exchange not only pre-figured the later clash between Snow and Leavis, but it also symbolised the ways in which social and institutional snobberies clustered around this topic. Although the two men themselves were good friends, they represented different worlds. Huxley's own social origins were relatively modest; he taught at a non-university vocational institution; he had been speaking at the opening of a commerce-directed college; and despite his great personal triumphs in the arena of High Victorian culture, he still represented a voice from outside the traditional centres of privilege and power. Arnold, by contrast, the son of Rugby's most famous headmaster, moved easily among the classical and European literatures, and wrote

[6] Matthew Arnold, 'Literature and Science' (1882), repr. in R.H. Super (ed.), *The Complete Prose Works of Matthew Arnold*, vol. x (Ann Arbor, 1974), pp. 52–73.

in a patrician literary style; he had come to be regarded as the incarnation of the Oxford whose charms he had memorably celebrated while Professor of Poetry there. Not for the last time in British cultural history, questions about the proper place of the sciences and the humanities in the nation's educational system appeared to be inextricably entangled with elusive but highly-charged matters of institutional status and social class. Arguably, the persistence of these social attitudes was to shape both Snow's later analysis and the response to it within Britain.[7]

Although the structure of education has changed considerably since Huxley and Arnold had their (notably amicable) exchange, the problem of academic specialisation and its consequences has continued to take a distinctive, and perhaps particularly acute, form in England. Both the final stages of school education and all of undergraduate university education have been more specialised there than in any comparable country. At the time of Snow's lecture, this pattern had assumed an extreme form: it was common for academically gifted children to start concentrating wholly upon science subjects or humanities subjects from as early as fourteen years old, to study only three of these subjects between sixteen and eighteen, and then to concentrate exclusively upon one while at university. In recent decades, some attempts have been made to allow a broader or more mixed choice of subjects at both school and university, but the situation in England still contrasts strikingly not only with the pattern in the United States, but also with those in other European countries, where a different inheritance of cultural attitudes as well

[7] See the historical survey in Hilary Rose and Steven Rose, *Science in Society* (London, 1969).

as of educational arrangements has given a distinctive inflection to the 'two cultures' theme. In France, for example, there has grown up an intimate connection between some of the leading scientific 'grandes écoles' and recruitment to the higher reaches of national administration and public life: many senior civil servants as well as financiers and industrialists are graduates of the immensely prestigious Ecole Polytechnique with qualifications in engineering. At a different level, the high reputation of the Technische Hochschule in Germany gives a vocationally oriented scientific education a greater social standing than it has ever had in Britain, and has helped to form a cadre of managers in industry and commerce who have impressive technical qualifications. The resonance of the 'two cultures' theme in these countries has inevitably been modified by these differing cultural traditions. But although the issue has come to acquire a certain autonomous existence, the form in which we now encounter it still bears the marks both of Snow's own concerns and of the controversies in which it immediately became embroiled, and it may be helpful to re-consider these historical circumstances in a little more detail.

Snow's life

Charles Percy Snow, the second of the four sons of William Edward Snow and Ada Sophia *née* Robinson, was born on 15 October 1905 in Leicester in the heart of the English midlands.[8] The family history of the male Snows encapsulated the main stages of the development of modern industrial England. The great-grandfather,

[8] The fullest source of biographical information is Philip Snow, *Stranger and Brother: A Portrait of C.P. Snow* (London, 1982).

John Snow, had been born in rural Devon in 1801, and though reportedly illiterate all his life, migrated as part of the first Industrial Revolution to the Birmingham area where he became an engine fitter. The grandfather, William Henry Snow, was a characteristic Victorian figure, a radical and nonconformist who educated himself and became foreman engineer of the Leicester tramways, supervising the replacement of horse-drawn by electric trams. He lived until 1916, incarnating for his elder grandsons the self-help and stern virtue of an heroic age (Charles was to refer to him with admiration several times in his writing and lectures). The father, William Edward Snow, had strong musical leanings: he was the organist at his parish church, and became an Associate and eventually a Fellow of the Royal College or Organists, a fact of which he was immensely proud. But music could not earn him a living; for that he worked as a clerk in a shoe factory in Leicester. In the delicate gradations of English class identities, the Snow family hovered just on the right side of that crucial divide between the would-be genteel lower-middle class and the barely respectable upper-working class. Financially, their situation was straitened and precarious, little different from that of the families of the bricklayers, warehousemen, and foremen stokers who occupied the surrounding, slightly inferior, terraced houses. But the Snows' house was semi-detached, the father gave piano lessons in the back parlour, and the sons were sent to a small private school rather than to the local Board school. Snow was to be intensely conscious of matters of social class throughout his life, a preoccupation and set of responses which were to leave their mark on his writing.

Charles Snow (know to his family as Percy until his

marriage in 1950 to the novelist Pamela Hansford Johnson) followed the classic route of the clever, bookish boy without social advantages: the local public library was a lifeline to a wider imaginative world, and from the age of eleven his intellectual, cultural, and sporting aspirations were encouraged at Alderman Newton's School in Leicester, a modest local grammar school founded in the eighteenth century. Alderman Newtons' was far from outstanding academically: in Snow's time nobody had managed to get to university directly from the school. Its strength was in science rather than in the traditionally more prestigious classics and humanities, and this was the area on which Snow concentrated. Although he distinguished himself, there were still gaps in the educational ladder up which he was climbing: despite successfully completing his Intermediate Examination in Science in 1923, he had to wait two years before he could begin to study for his degree, during which period he earned a pittance working as laboratory assistant at the school and feeding his mind with a wide range of reading, especially in the nineteenth-century European novel. In 1925 he became a student in the newly established Chemistry and Physics department of nearby Leicester University College, one of those small provincial centres of higher education which at the time were only allowed to award external London University degrees. Snow obtained a First in Chemistry in 1927 and an M.Sc. in 1928. He was an intensely ambitious young man who had worked so hard during his final year as to push himself to the verge of a physical breakdown. But he achieved the success he needed to make the decisive step into the wider world, winning scholarships which allowed him to enter Christ's College, Cambridge as a Ph.D. student in October 1928.

Snow began research in the field of infra-red spectroscopy in the by then world-famous Cavendish Laboratory headed by Lord Rutherford. His research prospered, and in 1930, at the age of twenty-five, he was elected a Fellow of Christ's College, a position he retained until 1945. At first, he seemed marked out for a successful career as a research scientist, but in 1932 he suffered a setback which re-directed his life. He and a colleague believed they had discovered how to produce Vitamin A by artificial methods. The discovery promised to be of immense theoretical and practical importance, and, following the announcement in *Nature*, the President of the Royal Society confirmed to the national press the significance of the findings. But alas, their calculations had been faulty, their 'discovery' had to be recanted amid considerable publicity, and, as his brother later put it, 'the trauma after all that publicity put Charles off scientific research irrevocably'.[9] That Snow was a trained scientist was crucial to the authority with which he was later to treat the question of the 'two cultures', but, as those scientists uneasy with this self-appointed champion of the scientific culture were to remark, his credentials were in fact somewhat shaky. By the time he came to give his Rede lecture, it was more than twenty years since he had been engaged in first-hand scientific research, and his achievement as a scientists had been patchy at best.

Two developments helped snow to carve out an alternative career for himself. In 1932 he published *Death Under Sail*, a detective story, followed two years later by *The Search*, a novel about a young scientist. These early efforts had been favourably reviewed, encouraging him to think of himself as a serious writer,

[9] Snow, *Stranger and Brother*, p. 35.

and at the beginning of 1935 he had the idea for a series of linked novels which were to become the eleven volumes of the 'Strangers and Brothers' sequence published between 1940 and 1970. There can be no doubt that Snow's later fame and public standing rested upon the success of these novels, which sold widely and were translated into several languages. But the source of the more immediately providential turn in his career was the outbreak of the Second World War. Snow was temporarily drafted into the Civil Service with responsibility for the recruitment and deployment of physical scientists to support the war effort. This gave scope for his administrative talents, helped him to form contacts with important people, and indulged his yearning to observe the exercise of power from the inside. In 1945 he decided not to return to Cambridge, but instead took up two part-time posts which would enable him to continue writing fiction: he became a Civil Service Commissioner, dealing principally with scientific appointments, and in private industry he occupied a largely advisory position, and ultimately a directorship, at the English Electric Company. Following the success of his novels, he was eventually able to give up these posts, and it was his release from the constraints of his official position in 1959 that allowed him to begin his third career as public figure, controversial lecturer, and pundit. The Rede lecture was the first, and by a long way the most famous, of his pronouncements in this new role.

The 1960s were the peak of Snow's reputation. Books were written about his novels and plays; he received twenty honorary degrees in the course of the decade; and, above all, the idea of the 'two cultures', the source of his greatest fame, became the basis for a minor

industry of comment and controversy. (It was noticeable that nearly all his honours came from foreign
universities, and his pronouncements were received in
other countries without those shafts of scepticism and
even scorn with which his otherwise enthusiastic recep-
tion in Britain was often shot through.) Following the
Labour Party's election victory in October 1964, he
accepted Harold Wilson's invitation to become the
second-in-command at the newly established Ministry
of Technology, taking a Life Peerage and becoming the
government spokesman on technology in the House of
Lords. He resigned his ministerial post in April 1966,
but thereafter he continued to sustain, and even
increase, his prolific literary output, both fiction and
non-fiction, and he travelled the world as lecturer,
adviser, and public sage, holding forth on the problems
of peace, poverty, and development. He died on 1 July
1980.

Development of the idea of the 'two cultures'

Many of the preoccupations which surfaced in the
controversy surrounding 'The Two Cultures and the
Scientific Revolution' now appear to belong distinc-
tively to the late 1950s and early 1960s. But in fact the
germ of the argument and the tone of the lecture can be
traced back to much earlier stages of Snow's career, and
to a surprising extent they reflect facets of Snow's
intellectual development which were shaped and fixed
in the 1930s. Snow himself always looked back to the
inter-war period, and especially to the Cambridge of the
1930s, as a Golden Age of original scientific research,
and he evidently imbibed a certain cultural conception
of science that was especially powerful in those years,

particularly among 'progressive' scientists and radical spokesmen for science such as J.D. Bernal and P.M.S. Blackett. He saw science as the great hope in a world which the traditional elites had mismanaged and led into economic depression and to the brink of a second devastating war. He also saw it as the one true meritocracy, in which sheer ability could overcome social disadvantages to obtain its true reward. And, in more parochial terms, the young Snow developed an antipathy to 'literary intellectuals', especially to what he identified as their snobbish and nostalgic social attitudes, which was never to leave him.

His apparent hankering for the rule of a scientific elite was one of the several grounds on which he was compared to the leading literary champion of science in the previous generation, H.G. Wells. In fact, Snow's early admiration for Wells provides one key to understanding the dynamics of the 'two cultures' controversy. A particularly revealing piece of evidence is the review of Wells's *Experiment in Autobiography* which Snow published in *The Cambridge Review* in 1934. Snow made clear that he admired Wells as 'a great writer' and 'a remarkable man', sympathising with his 'urge for a planned world', but he also indicated that he was irritated by the dismissive attitude towards Wells prevalent in Cambridge, especially among literary critics. Part of this attitude he attributed to the fact that Wells 'is the least nostalgic of great writers' ('he has deliberately spent much of his intelligence in making plans' for the future), and this early review already contains the seeds of his later attack on 'literary intellectuals' as 'natural Luddites'. Snow emphasised his scorn for such attitudes: 'if art be all gestures of futility, despair, and homesick escape, then Wells is less of an artist than anyone who ever wrote'.[10]

In fact, these differing responses to Wells constituted even more of a direct rehearsal for the controversy that was to erupt thirty years later than may be suggested by Snow's generalised irritation with the scornful attitude in Cambridge literary circles. For, in the very first number of *Scrutiny* in 1932, it was F.R. Leavis himself who reviewed Wells's latest book, *The Work, Wealth, and Happiness of Mankind*. Leavis was more than hostile, he was dismissive. Indeed, he doubted whether Wells was by now worth reviewing, but, in phrases uncannily anticipatory of his later assault on Snow, he argued that Wells had to be discussed 'as a case, a type, a portent. As such, he matters.' Leavis also rehearsed the same refrain about the limitations of the technocratic vision of human well-being: 'the efficiency of the machinery becomes the ultimate value, and this seems to us to mean something very different from expanding and richer human life'.[11] In the same issue, in his essay on 'the Literary Mind', Leavis had dismembered the American cultural commentator Max Eastman, and one of his most crushing rebukes was: 'He believes with implicit faith that [science] will settle all our problems for us. In short, he lives still in the age of H.G. Wells.'[12]

Snow's review of Wells contains unmistakable evidence that Leavis was one of the Cambridge critics he had in mind, not just in the reference to 'the opposition's' estimating T.S. Eliot (still a controversial and

[10] C.P. Snow, 'H.G. Wells and Ourselves', *The Cambridge Review*, 56 (19 Oct. and 30 Nov. 1934), 27–8, 148. Snow was much later to publish an admiring appreciation of Wells in his *Variety of Men* (London, 1967).

[11] F.R. Leavis, 'Babbitt Buys the World', *Scrutiny*, 1 (1932), 80, 82.

[12] F.R. Leavis, 'The Literary Mind', *Scrutiny*, 1 (1932), 30.

far from 'canonised' author at this date) above Wells, but also in his pointed sneer about the way 'undergraduates can be led to say that Gerard Manley Hopkins was the only justification for the nineteenth century'. Leavis was not only one of Eliot's earliest academic champions, but he was also constantly accused of indoctrinating his students with 'correct' literary judgements, and Hopkins had been the one nineteenth-century writer treated favourably and at length in Leavis's *New Bearings in English Poetry* which had appeared in 1932. Understandably, public figures often address tomorrow's problems with yesterday's attitudes, but it is perhaps especially striking to see how much of the later thinking of Snow, who prided himself on always looking forward and on being the spokesman for those who 'have the future in their bones', should have been shaped by the antagonisms of Cambridge in the 1930s.

Snow's concern with the cultural role and political impact of science continually surfaced in both his novels and his official work throughout the 1940s and 1950s, but the first public airing of his idea about the 'two cultures' was in a short article with that title in the *New Statesman* in October 1956 (a good many sentences from this article were to re-appear essentially unchanged in the Rede lecture). It is even clearer in this early piece than in the later extended version just how far the whole conception was animated by a hostility to a particular conception of 'literary intellectuals'.[13] 'The traditional culture, which is, of course, mainly literary, is behaving like a state whose power is rapidly declining – standing on its precarious dignity, spending far too much energy on

[13] Snow apparently cultivated a more general hostility to intellectuals: 'He is on record as saying that he preferred decent soldiers to indifferent intellectuals. For him an intelligent person rather than an intellectual every time.' Snow, *Stranger and Brother*, p.143.

Alexandrian intricacies, occasionally letting fly in fits of aggressive pique quite beyond its means, too much on the defensive to show any generous imagination to the forces which must inevitably reshape it.' Other aspects of Snow's hostility emerge only through innuendo: the tone of scientific culture, he observes, is 'steadily heterosexual'; unlike in the literary culture, 'there is an absence . . . of the feline and oblique'.[14]

This early version of the 'two cultures' thesis is also revealing in two further ways. First, and in sharp contrast to the context in which the topic has mostly been discussed subsequently, it is noticeable that Snow is not here concerned with the structure and content of educational arrangements; he is talking about characteristics of research scientists and of writers as groups, and makes no practical proposals for shrinking the gap he identifies between them. Second, unlike the Rede lecture, and still more Snow's later reflections upon what he was 'primarily' getting at in that famous performance, his 1956 article does not raise the question of the relations between the rich and poor countries and the problems involved in policy decisions about the application of technology by scientifically illiterate politicians and administrators. His chief theme in this article is his conviction of the greater 'moral health' of scientists as a group over 'literary intellectuals'. Scientists, he asserts, are by nature concerned about the collective welfare and future of humanity. The contrast with 'the traditional culture' is made by way of an extraordinarily tendentious selection of examples: 'Dostoyevski sucking up to

---

[14] C.P. Snow, 'The Two Cultures', *New Statesman* (6 Oct. 1956), 413.

the Chancellor Pobedonostsev who thought the only thing wrong with slavery was that there was not enough of it; the political decadence of the *avant-garde* of 1914, with Ezra Pound finishing up broadcasting for the Fascists; Claudel agreeing sanctimoniously with the Marshal about the virtue in others' suffering; Faulkner giving sentimental reasons for treating Negroes as a different species.' Such betrayals stemmed from the tendency of writers to let their perception of the tragic nature of individual life obscure the needs of their fellow human beings. From this attitude, 'made up of defeat, self-indulgence, and moral vanity, the scientific culture is almost totally immune'. The central message of this first sketch of 'the two cultures' is that 'the greatest enrichment the scientific culture could give us is . . . a moral one'.[15]

Two years later, in an article ostensibly discussing 'the age of Rutherford', Snow re-stated these themes (and again revealed just how rooted in the inter-war period the basic categories of his thinking were). The same contrasts recur: 'Between Rutherford and Blackett on the one hand, and, say, Wyndham Lewis and Ezra Pound on the other, who are on the side of their fellow human beings?' The literary figures were backward-looking, had 'ambiguous relations with Fascism', and were tainted with anti-Semitism, whereas, 'like all scientists, conservative or radical, [Rutherford] had, almost without thinking what it meant, the future in his

---

[15] *Ibid.*, 414. Snow developed further his conception of the inherently moralising nature of scientific research in 'The Moral Un-neutrality of Science', an address given to the American Association for the Advancement of Science in 1960, published in *Science* in 1961, and republished in his *Public Affairs* (London, 1971).

bones'.[16] The origins of some of the most puzzling or provocative aspects of the Rede lecture (as well as some of its key phrases) are evident in these earlier sketches, and above all they help us better to understand the damning characterisation of 'literary intellectuals' offered in that lecture – offered, it must be remembered, by a man who was at the time best known as a novelist. For as one sympathetic observer quizzically remarked of that later performance: 'There can be no other interpretation of his lecture than that it takes towards literature a position of extreme antagonism.'[17]

One final observation to be borne in mind when reading 'The Two Cultures and the Scientific Revolution' concerns the genre to which it belongs. A lecture is above all an occasion, in both senses of the word – it is a social event and it is an opportunity. The lecturer has been invited: he or she is licensed to pronounce. (It would be interesting to analyse just how many of the major controversies in modern culture have had their origins in some form of public lecture.) Though the published form may be the length of an essay, there is an important difference of tone and intention between it and something written as an essay. The lecture never quite manages the intimate, meditative, sometimes almost whimsical tone that marks the classic essay. The lecture strikes a more declarative or argumentative pose, and even though the best lectures exploit a collusive relation with their audience, the form is inherently pedagogic (not for nothing has *ex cathedra*, from the professor's chair, become synonomous with 'speaking with authority'). This was a tone that came easily to Snow. His

[16] C.P. Snow, 'The Age of Rutherford', *Atlantic Monthly*, 102 (1958), 79, 80.
[17] Lionel Trilling, 'The Leavis–Snow Controversy', reprinted in his *Beyond Culture: Essays on Literature and Learning* (New York, 1965), p.152. This essay first appeared as 'A Comment on the

writing constantly deploys the tropes of modesty to mask an assertion of authority: the manner is that of one who has weighed unmentioned evidence, who knows the grave consequences of getting it wrong, but who is better placed than anyone else to get it right.

In reading Snow's text, therefore, we need to remember its origins, and to accept that he was not a systematic thinker nor, in some ways, a particularly exact writer. His preferred ground was that of the Big Idea: he seized it, turned it in a somewhat unconventional direction, illustrated it with a few facts and anecdotes taken from widely differing domains, and reiterated it in accessible, forceful prose. As he became more famous, the idea tended to get bigger, the facts fewer, and the prose more forceful.[18] He aimed, above all, to attract attention to what he had to say. Judged by this criterion, the success of his Rede lecture must be beyond dispute.

Reactions and controversies

Although the notion of the 'two cultures' has attracted almost continuous comment, in some form or another, since Snow first articulated it, the earlier stages of response were naturally the most intense and the most revealing. One episode, in particular, stands out: the furore surrounding F.R. Leavis's ferocious attack on Snow and his lecture in 1962. This involved the clash of fundamentally opposed conceptions of how to think about human well-being, and, partly because it provoked the public expression of such strong feelings (and

Leavis–Snow Controversy', *Commentary* (1962), and it was also published in *University Quarterly*, 17 (1962), 9–32; Snow cites this essay at note 53 below, but ascribes it to 1959.

[18] This is most of all evident in the later pieces collected in *Public Affairs*, such as 'The State of Siege', delivered in 1968.

strong words), it has since been taken as emblematic of the very division Snow had attempted to identify.

The text of the Rede lecture was published in *Encounter* in two parts, in June and July 1959, and the August number then included a small symposium of immediate responses.[19] These reactions were overwhelmingly favourable, and Snow was praised for his 'brilliant' delineation of the divide between the cultures.[20] (The historian J.H. Plumb sounded a note of reservation, preferring to see the tensions which Snow had referred to as part of a larger social development, with the scientists as a new class threatening to displace the largely upper-middle-class literary elite that had held sway in the years from 1910 to 1950.) Moreover, it was clear that most of the respondents believed, implicitly or explicitly, that the pressing problem was to raise the status of science and to increase the scientific literacy of the non-scientists rather than vice versa. More broadly, the published form of the lecture attracted international comment, the general tendency of which was to congratulate Snow for having diagnosed an increasingly pressing modern problem.

In reflecting on the first wave of response, therefore,

[19] C.P. Snow, 'The Two Cultures and the Scientific Revolution', *Encounter*, 12 (June 1959), 17–24; 13 (July 1959), 22–7. '"The Two Cultures": a Discussion of C.P. Snow's Views', 13 (August 1959), 67–73, contained contributions from Walter Allen, Bernard Lovell, J.H. Plumb, David Riesman, Bertrand Russell, John Cockcroft, and Michael Ayrton.

[20] The brief communication from the 87-year-old Bertrand Russell claimed that the divide between the cultures was of fairly recent origin. He sought to support this claim by saying: 'Cartwright, who invented the power loom, was my grandfather's tutor and taught him to construe the odes of Horace', though he perhaps slightly weakened the force of the example by adding, 'so far as I have been able to discover, his invention of the power loom remained unknown to my grandfather' (71).

Snow felt he had good cause to be satisfied.[21] 'Just as the concept of the "two cultures" has been accepted, so has the existence of a gulf between them.' Indeed, Snow now wanted to press the case further: 'The division between the cultures is inherent in an advanced industrial society.' But again, though he now offered the occasional mild qualification, he returned to his central concern with the way in which major twentieth-century writers had encouraged an undiscriminating and ultimately selfish hostility to the 'industrial-scientific revolution' (he made clear that he saw the Industrial Revolution of the late-eighteenth century as only the first stage in an extended process of the application of science to production). Revealingly, he gave over the bulk of his 'reply' (for such it effectively was) to re-stating this case against criticisms of his optimistic technologism by literary and cultural critics (such as G.H. Bantock, a old Scrutineer[22]). After this, the attention Snow's thesis received began to die down, but this proved to be only the lull before a remarkable polemical storm.

F.R. Leavis was due to retire from his post as University Reader in English at Cambridge in the summer of 1962. For more than thirty years he had been one of the most distinctive, controversial, and influential literary critics in the English-speaking world, though he had long chafed at what he felt was a lack of due recognition (his own university, for example, had only promoted him three years before his retirement). With an intensity which often shaded into ferocity his

[21] C.P. Snow, 'The "Two Cultures" Controversy: Afterthoughts', *Encounter*, 14 (Feb. 1960), 64–8.
[22] G.H. Bantock, 'A Scream of Horror', *The Listener* (17 Sept. 1959), 427–8.

criticism had attempted to vindicate the claims of 'great' literature (he was not much interested in any other kind) to be a unique and living repository of the most vital, in every sense, human responses. In the complex, deeply-felt experience enacted in these incomparable works of the imagination he saw an antidote, now the only possible antidote, to the cheapening and corrupting of experience which the dominant forces of modern mass society conspired to promote. The criticism and teaching of English literature, therefore, presented itself to Leavis as a calling of awesome and almost sacred responsibility. For the trivial or self-serving or merely fashionable he had no tolerance whatsoever – his combination of puritan earnestness and passionate sense of the lateness of the hour ruled out compromise and coexistence – and fewer and fewer people or books were safe from his scarifying contempt as he became increasingly embittered and beleaguered. This was the man whom the students at Downing, his own college in Cambridge, invited to give the Richmond lecture in 1962. Leavis had not yet made a public pronouncement on Snow's 'two cultures' thesis: he now did so to such effect that the whole episode is still often referred to as 'the Snow–Leavis controversy'.[23]

In retrospect, one can only feel that a malevolent deity setting out to design a single figure in whom the largest number of Leavis's deepest antipathies would find themselves embodied could not have done better than to create Charles Percy Snow. There can never have been any question about Leavis's opinion of Snow's novels. Leavis's disdain for writing he regarded as superficial,

[23] See the material collected in David K. Cornelius and Edwin St Vincent (eds.), *Cultures in Conflict: Perspectives on the Snow-Leavis Controversy* (Chicago, 1964).

mechanical, or merely popular was boundless. That Snow's novels enjoyed, in the late 1940s and 1950s, a considerable *réclame* in the London literary world was, in Leavis's eyes, further damning evidence of their meretriciousness. And that world, the world of 'literary London', of smart cocktail parties, of reviews in the Sunday papers, of the latest 'view' propounded in the *New Statesman* or on the BBC's Third Programme, was a world in which Snow had come to move easily and with increasing fame. But Snow was also a technocrat, a spokesman for what Leavis regarded as the 'technologico-Benthamite' reduction of human experience to the quantifiable, the measurable, the manageable. And Snow had blundered across one of the most sensitive terrains in twentieth-century English culture: the assessment of the human consequences of the Industrial Revolution.

Leavis's contempt was total. He began by drawing attention to Snow's unargued assumption of authority and his striking complacency of tone – 'a tone of which one can say that, while only genius could justify it, one cannot readily think of genius adopting it'. Far from being a genius, Snow 'is intellectually as undistinguished as it is possible to be'; his lecture 'exhibits an utter lack of intellectual distinction and an embarrassing vulgarity of style'; 'the intellectual nullity is what constitutes any difficulty there may be in dealing with Snow's panoptic pseudo-cogencies', and so on. Leavis rightly perceived that part of what had led Snow to be regarded as a credible authority on the 'two cultures' was his dual identity as man of science and successful novelist. To discredit this presumption of authority, Leavis felt he had to make uncomfortably clear just where Snow's novels stood in the scale of literature, and here his attack seemed to most observers to become unjustifiably *ad hominem*. 'Snow is, of course, a – no, I can't say that; he isn't; Snow thinks of himself as a novelist', but 'as a novelist he doesn't exist; he doesn't begin to exist. He can't be said to know what a novel is. The nonentity is apparent on every page of his fictions', and more in the same vein. In two paragraphs Leavis gave a devastating picture of what he (though not, it should be said, he alone) saw as the weaknesses of Snow's fiction – its characterless, unspeakable dialogue, its constant resort to telling rather than showing, and its limited imaginative range. Even, he added (and surely not without some justice), when Snow is depicting the world he is supposed to know best, that of academic life, he represents it in a way that empties it of its main intellectual activity and sustaining purpose. Nor was Leavis willing to allow Snow the benefit of the authority of science. The Rede lecture contains, he insisted remorselessly, no evidence of actual scientific training or habits of mind; instead of rigour, there is just 'a show of knowledgeableness'.[24]

Leavis treated Snow's fame as a symptom, a 'portent', of how contemporary society had largely lost the ability to frame anything like an adequate description of the values which could give life a meaning. The language of 'prosperity' and 'rising standards of living' had come to fill this void, and Snow was the prophet of the consumer society. Leavis was particularly incensed that Snow, who appeared unshakeably confident of the benefits of industrialisation, should have dismissed as

[24] F.R. Leavis, 'Two Cultures? The Significance of C.P. Snow', *Spectator* (9 Mar. 1962), repr. as 'Two Cultures? The Significance of Lord Snow', in his *Nor Shall My Sword: Discourses on Pluralism, Compassion and Social Hope* (London, 1972), quotations at pp. 42, 44–5, 47.

'Luddites' those nineteenth-century authors who had raised doubts about the human cost of the Industrial Revolution. Coming, often partially and uneasily, to terms with the changes ushered in by the Industrial Revolution has arguably been the central drama at the heart of English culture for at least 150 years. To someone like Leavis (though there really was no one *like* him; he was the least 'representative' of men) one of the chief glories of English writers during this time had been their anguished sense of the profound damage inflicted by this development on the quality of experience. In 'A Second Look', Snow revealed his impatience with such fastidious nose-holding: historically the poor have always voted with their feet to go into factories as soon as the opportunity has offered, and the greatest hope for the poor countries of the world now was to extend the material benefits of industrialism. [25]

The 'Leavis–Snow controversy' can obviously be seen as a re-enactment of a familiar clash in English cultural history – the Romantic versus the Utilitarian, Coleridge versus Bentham, Arnold versus Huxley, and other less celebrated examples. And in this kind of cultural civil war, each fresh engagement is freighted with the weight of past defeats, past atrocities; for this reason there is always more at stake than the ostensible cause of the current dispute. But Leavis's attack might also be seen as an illustration of the specific case Snow wanted to make against 'literary intellectuals'. Many observers were puzzled as well as appalled by the

---

[25] Snow had read Raymond Williams's *Culture and Society*, published in 1958 (the quotation from Coleridge on p.62 below is surely taken from Williams, p.77), but its complex discussion of the literary responses to industrialism does not seem to have modified Snow's conviction that the champions of 'culture' were all tainted with 'Luddism'.

savagery of Leavis's criticisms, and could only explain it to themselves in terms of some personal motive such as envy or malice. This, however, was an unnecessary as well as implausible explanation. Leavis's uncompromising temperament played its part, as did his conviction that he had to be outspoken if he was to get the essential issues attended to – and the essential issues included the nature of Snow's authority and tone. But beyond that, Leavis's attack needs to be understood as an example of something much deeper about the assumptions underlying a certain kind of literary criticism.

The literary critic, habitually attending to the fine texture of verbal detail, can at times barely be persuaded that something is being said at all if it is being said badly. It is almost a truism of the critic's working practice that the conventional distinction between form and content is misleading in literature: a work is those words in that order – one cannot blithely assume some 'meaning' behind them which failed to get itself expressed properly but which is nonetheless the 'message' of the text. The critic thus seizes on the poverty of thought that is betrayed by slack, confused, empty writing, finding evidence of, ultimately, poverty of being. Such writing is at best a symptom of an incapacity; it can hardly be granted the dignity of fully intended expression. As a result, the literary critic frequently seems to the disinterested observer to be exaggerating the *personal* failings of the author or critic under scrutiny, and neglecting the content of what was being, however ineptly or unclearly, said. This is not the least important source of that spirit of *ad hominem* animosity that appals outsiders in literary-critical polemics.

Leavis's response to Snow corresponds to this pattern. Some of his strictures on the flaccid, crudely approximate quality of Snow's prose were not without justification, and some of his judgements about the limited imagination and sheer perceptual carelessness revealed by such writing had a point and a general relevance. But what it was in Snow's lecture that stirred so many in such a variety of different cultural situations to feel that he had put his finger on or helpfully near a major topic of concern – this Leavis's allergic reaction to Snow's writing prevented him from estimating fairly.

Leavis's attack provoked outcry, though from this distance the fuss seems to have been as much about good manners as good arguments. The text of Leavis's lecture was published in the *Spectator* on 9 March 1962 (a reminder that this debate about modernity was conducted through those two traditional genres, the lecture and the periodical essay). The next issue contained no fewer than sixteen letters on the topic, nearly all condemning Leavis's excesses, and a further fifteen letters were published the following week. The spate of letters continued, with an increasing number supporting Leavis, and on 30 March the *Spectator* carried an editorial which concentrated on criticising Snow for seeming to suggest that science provided sufficient light by which to steer the world.[26] Not the least interesting of the letters came from the Cambridge theologian, Charles Raven, the acknowledged model for the character of Paul Jago in Snow's best-known novel, *The Masters*. Raven's letter was dignified but dismissive, remarking

[26] The editorial mischievously quoted William James: 'Of all the insufficient authorities as to the total nature of reality, give me the "scientists" . . . Their interests are most incomplete and their professional conceit and bigotry immense. I know of no narrower sect or club, in spite of their excellent authority in the line of fact they have explored, and their splendid achievements there.' *Spectator* (30 Mar. 1962), 387.

that Snow's novels revealed that he did not understand the nature of the academic pursuits about which he presumed to pontificate in his lecture: instead, 'Sir Charles offers us only careerism. That is the case against him.'[27]

But the most telling, and subsequently much the most widely cited, comment on the whole episode came from the leading American literary and cultural critic Lionel Trilling, and it was all the more telling because his reputation for wide-ranging and urbane reflectiveness, together with his elegant gravity of manner meant that his remarks could not be dismissed as merely polemical or partisan. Not surprisingly, he objected to Leavis's tone: 'There can be no two opinions about the tone in which Dr Leavis deals with Sir Charles. It is a bad tone, an impermissible tone.' But although in this and other ways Trilling distanced himself from Leavis's attack, it became clear in the course of his essay that he thought Leavis's criticisms were more right than wrong. In particular, Trilling concentrated upon what he saw as the slide in Snow's lecture from the views of a few major Modernist writers to 'literary intellectuals' or 'literature' in general, and then, more culpably still, from that to 'the traditional culture', culminating in Snow's key claim that 'it is the traditional culture, to an extent remarkably little diminished by the emergence of the scientific one, which manages the western world' (p. 11 below). But by this point the implied equivalence between the views of a few Modernist writers and the management of the Western world looks implausibly strained – or as the normally restrained Trilling put it: 'It is a bewildering statement.' What could Snow mean by talking of 'traditional culture' in this way? 'That this

[27] *Spectator* (6 Apr. 1962), 443.

culture, as we agree to call it, is *literary*, that it bears the same relation to actual literary men and their books that what is called the "scientific culture" bears to scientists and their work in laboratories, is truly a staggering thought.' Trilling also took issue, as Leavis had, with Snow's complaint that the nineteenth-century men of letters had either regretted the Industrial Revolution or ignored it: 'Nothing could be further from the truth.'[28]

Trilling surmised that the contradictions and exaggerations of Snow's lecture could only be explained by Snow's over-riding pursuit of an aim which distorted his judgement of other matters, and that this aim was the possibility of furthering East–West relations, and hence world peace, through the mutual understanding which communities of scientists in the two parts of the world could find. But in this Trilling found another of the defects of Snow's lecture: 'It communicates the strongest possible wish that we should forget about politics.' Trilling's conclusion was characteristically even-handed: 'I take *The Two Cultures* to be a book which is mistaken in a very large way indeed', he wrote, but he also judged Leavis's response to be 'parochial'. Indeed, Trilling's shrewdest point depended upon the sense of perspective which cultural distance brings, for he emphasised how much the two antagonists had in common. They came from comparable social backgrounds, standing outside the traditional social elites, and they represented two facets of a common ethos: 'A lively young person of advanced tastes would surely say that if ever two men were committed to England,

[28] Trilling, 'The Leavis–Snow Controversy', pp. 150, 156, 158. Trilling's interpretation of Snow's argument on these matters was challenged by Martin Green, 'Lionel Trilling and the Two Cultures', *Essays in Criticism*, 13 (1963), 375–85, and Snow cites Green's objection at note 53 below.

Home, and Duty, they are Leavis and Snow.' In this sense, they were both 'Roundheads'.[29]

Only in 1970 did Snow directly address Leavis's attacks, prompted by a further lecture by Leavis which was reprinted in *The Times Literary Supplement*. Snow made clear that he felt Leavis had broken the ground-rules of debate – had misquoted him, had attributed to him opinions he did not hold, had made statements which were demonstrably untrue. But by this point, the debate had become inextricably entangled with the question of the expansion of higher education in Britain. Snow had applauded the establishment of new universities in the early 1960s; he had endorsed the expansionist principles of the Robbins Report of 1963; and during his brief period in government he had been instrumental in furthering the establishment of Colleges of Advanced Technology. He had thus become publicly identified with a policy of vigorous expansion at a point when critics objected that 'more means worse', that expansion could only be achieved at the cost of falling standards. Leavis saw this expansion as making it less rather than more likely that his idea of the distinctive civilising role of the university in society would be realised, and again took Snow as representative of the mentality that conceived human needs in such instrumental and merely quantitive terms. This issue, and almost exactly these terms of dispute, have subsequently come to the surface in Britain with each successive modification of the education system, and illustrate further how the idea of the divide between

[29] Trilling, 'The Leavis–Snow Controversy', pp.163, 165, 171. Trilling also observed that Leavis 'has, as is well known, sympathy with very few modern writers, and he therefore cannot in good grace come to their defense against Sir Charles's characterisation of them'.

'the two cultures' has become entangled with broader social and even moral attitudes.

A larger social development was also in play here, and, as so often in recent British history, matters of class were at the heart of it. Snow was clearly frustrated at the extent to which a traditionally educated upper class continued to dominate public life in Britain. His writing constantly urged the virtues of a meritocracy, above all a 'new class' of scientifically trained administrators who were unencumbered by traditional social attitudes. His 1956 article and the Rede lecture itself made plain that he himself was *socially* much more at ease in the company of scientists, and these writings are edged with some of the class *ressentiment* which is familiar in many of the novelists and playwrights of the 1950s.

In other ways, too, Snow's thesis and the responses it evoked belonged to a particular period of British political and cultural history. The end of the 1950s were 'the Sputnik years', in which military and economic anxieties were displaced onto the issue of technological competitiveness, and this in turn, as in Harold Wilson's famous 1964 election speech about 'the white heat of the technological revolution', was presented as a charter for 'modernising' Britain. Another book from much the same period that also attracted considerable attention was *The Crisis in the Humanities* edited by Snow's friend, J.H. Plumb (a book which is pervaded by references to Snow's thesis set in the context of these larger social anxieties).[30] The traditional conception of the humanities, argued Plumb, belonged to the education of a gentleman, fitting him for membership of the governing class. This was now socially out-dated, and the

[30] Several of the essayists refer to Snow's thesis, and Graham Hough hung his essay 'Crisis in Literary Education' on the Snow–Leavis

humanities needed to 'adapt themselves to the needs of a society dominated by science and technology'. Like Snow, Plumb associated science, democracy, and modernity together, and Britain fell short on all three. 'What is needed is less reverence for tradition and more humility towards the educational systems of those two great countries – America and Russia – which have tried to adjust their teaching to the urban, industrial world of the twentieth century.'[31] This is the authentic voice of the 'modernising' element in Britain in the early 1960s: neither its confidence nor its preferred models look quite so compelling thirty years later. Laments about archaic, gentlemanly cultural values obstructing 'modernisation' in Britain are themselves part of a long and still vigorous British tradition, and the danger, as the years since Snow's death chillingly demonstrate, is that they mainly succeed in giving ideological comfort to the most reductive kind of commercial philistinism.[32]

Snow himself always claimed to attribute the sheer volume of response his lecture elicited to the fact of his having brought into slightly clearer focus something that was already a vague or not wholly realised concern in most modern societies. Certainly, the scale of the response indicates that this was no merely parochial

controversy; J.H. Plumb (ed.), *Crisis in the Humanities* (Harmondsworth, 1964), esp. pp.96–7.

[31] Plumb (ed.), *Crisis in the Humanities*, pp.7–10. Plumb, six years Snow's junior, had followed the same route from modest social origins via Alderman Newton's School, Leicester, to Christ's College, Cambridge, of which he was eventually to become Master.

[32] See, for example, the controversy surrounding Martin Wiener, *English Culture and the Decline of the Industrial Spirit 1850–1980* (Cambridge, 1981), and the longer perspective provided by James Raven, 'British History and the Enterprise Culture', *Past and Present*, 123 (1989), 178–204.

British concern,[33] and in 'A Second Look' he emphasised its connection with global issues of poverty and
overpopulation. But his thesis about 'the two cultures'
has outlived the circumstances of its origins, and even a
brief examination of how well the central notion has
worn must look both at the changing map of academic
disciplines and at developments in the wider world.

The changing map of the disciplines

At the heart of the concept of the 'two cultures' is a
claim about academic disciplines. Other matters are
obviously intimately involved – questions of educational structure, social attitudes, government policy-
making and so on. But if the concept is to possess any
continuing persuasiveness it must offer an illuminating
characterisation of the divide between two sorts of
intellectual enquiry. It will already be clear that Snow's
notion cannot be taken as a wholly accurate represen-
tation of the state of the disciplines in 1959. Even if one
allows that he really had a more particular point to make
about the contrast between a set of largely backward-
looking or pessimistic attitudes associated with Modernist literature and a set of more optimistic and
'modernising' commitments associated with natural
science, and even if one sympathises with his strictures
on English social snobberies and the attitudes they
perpetuated in education, one would still be bound to

[33] The Cambridge University Press's file of reviews of the original
lecture, and especially of its re-issue in 1964 with 'A Second Look',
amply documents the world-wide interest in the theme. Snow
himself ruefully observed that 'it is frustrating to be told that some
of the more valuable discussions have been taking place in languages
not accessible to most Englishmen, such as Hungarian, Polish, and
Japanese' (p. 54 below).

enter many reservations about the notion's descriptive value, as of course his critics did. Thus, to turn to consider how things have changed since Snow's lecture is not at all to take his analysis as an unproblematic starting-point. But insofar as his central idea has lost some of its purchase in the intervening decades, this is due not just to the inevitable processes of concept-fatigue, but also to several significant intellectual and social changes.

In general terms, the most marked changes to the map of the disciplines in the last three decades have taken the apparently contradictory, or at least conflicting, forms of the sprouting of ever more specialised sub-disciplines and the growth of various forms of inter-disciplinary endeavour. But in one sense, these changes both tell in the same direction: in place of the old apparently confident empires, the map shows many more smaller states with networks of alliance and communication between them criss-crossing in complex and sometimes surprising ways. It is largely a matter of emphasis whether one regards these changes as indicating that, rather than two cultures, there are in fact two hundred and two cultures or that there is fundamentally only one culture. The difference between these two responses derives in part from accentuating different features of the idea of 'a culture'. The first concentrates on the intellectual equivalent of the micro-climate, and hence on how a plurality of largely self-contained enterprises, each with its own idiom and references points, sustain the ways of life of separate professional groups. The second looks, rather, for the largest common frame, the ways in which the various intellectual activities could be said to take part in a shared conversation or to exhibit certain common mental operations.

However, neither of these responses strictly rules out

the possibility of there still being something distinctive shared by those activities which are referred to as 'the sciences', and not characteristic of those designated 'the humanities', even if we do not take this to signal a structuring divide in intellectual life. In practice, it is clear that we still find it convenient to go on using terms like 'the humanities' and 'the sciences', and for most purposes we roughly know what we mean by them. But this conventional usage is not now underpinned by any agreed definitional criteria – it has become a matter of lively debate whether we should even be trying to identify any one method of enquiry or one range of subject-matter or one professional or cultural ethos as distinguishing 'science' from 'non-science'. There is, of course, a rich and illuminating history of attempts to establish the basis for such a distinction, attempts which flourished with particular abundance once the nineteenth century had endowed the category of science with the prestige and burden of being the only provider of reliable, objective knowledge. Philosophers such as Wilhelm Dilthey in the late-nineteenth century or Karl Popper in the mid-twentieth endeavoured to draft the relevant conceptual legislation, stipulating the general properties needing to be possessed by a form of knowledge or mode of enquiry before it could legitimately be designated 'scientific'. However, none of these attempts has ever commanded general assent, least of all among other philosophers of science. The activities conventionally referred to as 'the sciences' do not, it is argued, all proceed by experimental methods, do not all cast their findings in quantifiable form, do not all pursue falsification, do not all work on 'nature' rather than human beings; nor are they alone in seeking to produce general laws, replicable results, and cumulative knowledge.

As always with such definitional questions, we need to be alert to the different purposes for which we might wish to distinguish some activities as 'science' and others as 'non-science'. In the second half of the nineteenth century, in the heyday of the scientistic aspiration, this could mean discriminating those enquiries whose methods gave us 'real' knowledge from those which did not. Many practising scientists continue implicitly to endorse this assumption, and occasionally a self-appointed spokesman for science will articulate it in its most arrogantly imperial form. But such confident and blinkered positivism may now enjoy less cultural authority than it once did, and it has become more widely accepted that different forms of intellectual enquiry quite properly furnish us with a variety of kinds of knowledge and understanding, no one of which constitutes *the* model to which all the others should seek to conform.

Of course, just as the actual practice of research scientists has been little affected by the philosophers' various re-descriptions of their activities, so the popular understanding of the identity of 'scientists' has not been greatly troubled by these developments either. Common usage applies the term without hesitation to mathematicians, physicists, chemists, biologists, and to those conducting research in the domains of medicine, computing, and engineering. And even within universities, definitional questions usually only arise at the margins, and then often for some purely organisational or statistical purpose – should experimental psychologists be eligible for support from a particular scientific funding agency, should the work of demographers be included in returns for the geography department or the statistics department, and so on.

Nonetheless, even if the broad usage of the category 'science' has remained reasonably stable over recent decades, there have been changes both in the sciences themselves and, perhaps more significantly, in the understanding of science that bear upon Snow's 'two cultures' claim. In terms of its impact upon research in a wide range of fields, the development of molecular biology has probably been the most significant change in the face of science since the 1950s, re-defining whole areas of enquiry between biochemistry and medical research, and throwing up a host of vexed ethical and practical issues in bio-technology and genetic engineering. But in terms of the more general image of the nature of scientific thinking, it is probably work in theoretical physics, astronomy, and cosmology that has attracted most attention. Physics had long been seen, as it effectively was by Snow, as the hardest of the 'hard sciences', a kind of gold standard against which weaker or debased forms of science could be measured (their condition often being diagnosed as 'physics-envy'). Traditionally, physics was taken to exemplify how rigorously deductive analysis of a few general laws, confirmed or falsified by induction from controlled experiment, provided predictive knowledge of the behaviour of the physical properties of the universe.

The so-called 'new physics' of the last twenty years has modified this model in two related ways. First, its actual findings about the nature of matter or the origins of the universe appear to install unpredictability, open-endedness, and even an element of teleology into the very heart of our knowledge of the physical world. Developments in quantum physics and 'chaos theory' have even been taken to mark 'the death of materialism', that is, of the mechanistic model of the properties and

xlvii

behaviour of matter which had been dominant since Newton (a dramatisation of the implications of this work which many working in these fields would reject).[34] Secondly, the very nature of the revolutionary work in theoretical physics, astronomy, and cosmology has helped to challenge the model of scientific thinking which represented it as proceeding by a combination of rigorous deduction and controlled inferences from empirical observation. The role of imagination, of metaphor and analogy, of category-transforming speculation and off-beat intuitions has come to the fore much more (some would argue that these had always had their place in the actual processes of scientific discovery, whatever the prevailing account of 'scientific method'). As a result, more now tends to be heard about the similarity rather than the difference of mental operations across the science/humanities divide, even though some of the similarities, it must be said, seem to be of a rather strained or at best analogical kind.

In the academic world, the non-scientist's understanding of the nature and social role of science has probably been more significantly influenced by the work of historians, philosophers, and sociologists of science than by changes within science itself. In numerical and institutional terms, the history and philosophy of science was a fairly modest enterprise in Snow's time, but it has been a major academic growth area in recent decades. Work in this field has helped to make available a richer understanding of science, but it has also challenged some of the scientists' own cherished conceptions about themselves and their activities. Historians of

[34] The term 'the death of materialism' is taken from a recent popular summary of these developments by Paul Davies and John Gribbin, *The Matter Myth: Beyond Chaos and Complexity* (Harmondsworth,

science such as, notably, Thomas Kuhn have argued that scientific change does not invariably take the form of a steady accumulation of knowledge within stable parameters; 'anomalies' in the evidence accumulate to the point where change takes the form of a discontinuous jump or 'paradigm shift', which involves a fundamental change of perspective and the creation of a new professional consensus, which is itself largely rooted in generational change.[35] A broader programme of the social history of science has concentrated attention upon the role of 'external' factors, such as the class origins of scientists themselves, the political and cultural forces steering research in some directions rather than others, and the social and psychological needs catered to by ideals of professionalism and disinterestedness. More radically still, much recent work has been devoted to showing how the very constitution of scientific knowledge itself is dependent upon culturally variable norms and practices; seen in this way, 'science' is merely one set of cultural activities among others, as much an expression of a society's orientation to the world as its art or religion, and equally inseparable from fundamental issues of politics and morality.[36]

The broader impact of work of this kind has also

1992). For a more cautious and tough-minded account, which emphasises the role of experimental and observational evidence, see Malcolm S. Longair, 'Modern Cosmology: a Critical Assessment', *Quarterly Journal of the Royal Astronomical Society* 34 (1993).

[35] Thomas Kuhn, *The Structure of Scientific Revolutions* (Chicago, 1963 (2nd edn 1970); see also the discussion of Kuhn's work in Gary Gutting (ed.), *Paradigms and Revolutions: Appraisals and Applications of Thomas Kuhn's Philosophy of Science* (Notre Dame, Ill., 1980).

[36] The extensive recent literature is helpfully surveyed in Jan Golinski, 'The Theory of Practice and the Practice of Theory: Sociological Approaches in the History of Science', *Isis*, 81 (1990), 492–505.

owed something to the way its spirit has chimed with that of other currents that have enjoyed a certain prominence in recent decades, particuarly within the academic world. Some feminists, for example, have argued for the gender-specific nature of the ideals of control and impersonality enshrined in science, and have attacked the 'masculinist' bias of the conception of rationality to which the ideology of science appeals. The hugely fashionable enterprise of 'literary theory' has similarly reached out to subsume science under its characteristically corrosive categories: science, too, it is argued, is a discourse, involving the same kinds of rhetorical strategies, literary tropes, and unstable meanings as other forms of writing.[37] The cumulative tendency of these various approaches has been summed up by the German social theorist, Wolf Lepenies: 'Science must no longer give the impression it represents a faithful reflection of reality. What it is, rather, is a cultural system, and it exhibits to us an alienated interest-determined image of reality specific to a definite time and place.'[38] The radical implications of this recent work have certainly not been embraced by all historians and philosophers of science, let alone by practising research scientists. It may be that the pendulum of intellectual fashion will soon swing back towards a greater emphasis on the special status of scientific knowledge, but for the present the diffusion of such relativistic accounts of science has made it more difficult to endorse the starker or more aggressive version of the 'two cultures' thesis.

[37] For a representative recent example, see David Locke, *Science as Writing* (New Haven, 1992).

[38] Wolf Lepenies, 'The Direction of the Disciplines: the Future of the Universities', *Comparative Criticism*, 11 (1989), 64; here, in an article originally written in German, Lepenies is using the term

The fact that some of the trends just mentioned stemmed from recent work in the heartland of the humanities indicates that we also have to attend to changes on the other side of Snow's divide. It is sometimes forgotten that in his sketch of the culture of the 'literary intellectuals', Snow was not primarily talking about an academic group, but about writers and critics whose natural milieu was that of metropolitan publishing and journalism. His preferred shorthand for this milieu was 'Chelsea and Greenwich Village' not 'Oxford and Harvard' (e.g. p. 2 below). This obviously reflected the worlds with which Snow himself was most familiar, but it also points to a major change that has taken place in the intervening period and which has conditioned our understanding of the 'two cultures' idea. There has not only been a huge expansion of higher education across the world since the late 1950s, as a result of which universities and their concerns bulk larger in the national cultures of the advanced societies than they did; but there has also been a decline in the opportunities offered by these societies to make a living as a writer and literary journalist. Snow's 'literary culture' was chiefly composed of those who met each other at publishers' parties and who discussed the latest reviews of each other's work in the pages of the *New Statesman* or the *Partisan Review*. Since then, many of the periodicals of general culture have folded or sharply contracted their coverage of literature, and the modern counterparts to Snow's 'literary intellectuals' are more likely to meet each other at an academic conference or a campus-based 'writers' workshop'.

Moreover, Snow's highly selective characterisation of

'science' in its German sense of *Wissenschaft*, that is, any systematic body of enquiry.

the values represented by 'literature' now looks less persuasive than ever. The mixture of formal experimentalism with political reaction exhibited in much of High Modernism naturally provoked the hostility of someone who combined the positivist progressivism of the 1930s with a pre- or anti-Modernist fictional technique, and even when, in his first 'afterthought', he conceded that he had been selective in his description of 'literary intellectuals', he still maintained that this strain had 'dominated literary sensibility'.[39] This claim cannot be sustained in the face of the literature of the last thirty years; indeed, in some ways a mixture of traditional narrative techniques and limited, even parochial, subject-matter, not unlike that displayed in Snow's own novels, may have been more characteristic of writing in Britain during this period. Still less does the literature written in other parts of the world seem suffused with the reactionary or 'Luddite' tendencies that Snow deplored in Pound, Eliot, Wyndham Lewis and company. In passing one may remark a certain sadness in Snow that 'progressive', egalitarian, modernity-welcoming attitudes did not seem to have found expression in literature of anything like the power and appeal which the contrary values had done; there may have been deeper questions here about the memory-powered tendencies of the imagination than he allowed.

In shifting attention to the literary disciplines, it has to be recognised that it is criticism, not literature, that corresponds to science (literature, strictly speaking, corresponds to nature, the subject-matter of study). The academic face of literary study has changed with controversy-provoking rapidity since Snow's time, especially in the United States; indeed, the move away

[39] 'The "Two Cultures" Controversy: Afterthoughts', 66.

from explicitly evaluative criticism and towards a form of 'theory' has been seen by those unsympathetic to the changes as an example of the misguided aping of the procedures and claims of science. One of the most significant changes here, given the terms of Snow's initial contrast, has been the development, especially but not exclusively in the United States, of a whole sub-field or 'interdiscipline' of 'science and literature', with its own professional association and specialised publications.[40] Of course, in all such inter- or bi-disciplinary enterprises, the function of the conjunction is problematic: sometimes it represents mere juxtaposition, two proud kingdoms lying alongside in chaste self-sufficiency, but more often it connotes the subordination of one partner's subject-matter to the concerns of the other. In practice, scientists have not been rushing to apply their experimental techniques to the illumination of the plays of Shakespeare or the novels of Jane Austen, but literary theorists have been eager to extend the domain of discourse analysis to uncover the surprising figurative play at the heart of even the baldest scientific research paper. It is perhaps too soon to say whether such unions will produce offspring that are a joy to both parents, but the very attempt may have helped to lessen the gulf of incomprehension implied in the 'two cultures' thesis.

[40] There is now an international Society of Literature and Science, and separate bibliographies of the growing body of work in the field have been published; see 'Editor's Introduction' in the special issue on 'Literature and Science' of *Comparative Criticism*, 13 (1991), xv-xxix; for a representative sample of such work, see George Levine (ed.), *One Culture: Essays in Science and Literature* (Madison, 1987); and a special significance attaches to the first lecture on literature and science sponsored by the Royal Society, the British Academy, and the Royal Society of Literature: Gillian Beer, 'Translation or Transformation? The Relations of Literature

In 'A Second Look' Snow regretted that he had not sufficiently acknowledged the existence of what he was tempted to call the 'third culture', which he (prompted, it would seem, by J.H. Plumb) took to be represented by social historians. This was a rather feeble attempt to remedy an obvious omission in the original lecture which appeared to allow no place on its sketch-map of the disciplines for the social sciences. The characteristics Snow claimed to find in 'literary intellectuals' hardly seemed to be shared by economists or criminologists, yet he was clearly not including these disciplines in his category of science. It is true that in the late 1950s most universities in Britain had not yet been as welcoming to the newer social sciences as comparable institutions elsewhere, especially in the United States, but this is again an area which has seen enormous expansion since that period. On the whole, the dominant assumptions in many of these fields have become somewhat less positivist and have allowed greater room for more hermeneutic or simply historical modes of cultural analysis, but it is still the case that the professional ideals and forms of publication in many of the social sciences have at least as much in common with their neighbours in the natural sciences as with those in the humanities. In addition, there are now a very substantial number of academics who are engaged in various social, applied, professional, and vocational disciplines which cannot be classed as either 'humanities' or 'science', and for whom the notion of 'the two cultures' is, at best, an irrelevant anachronism.

As the examples mentioned in the foregoing paragraphs should remind us, various classifications of the

and Science', *Notes and Records of the Royal Society of London*, 44 (1990), 81–99.

disciplines are possible depending on which of their characteristics are chosen for comparison – classification in terms of subject-matter will produce a different grouping from classification in terms of form of publication, and so on. Reflection on this point should do more than simply soften Snow's original polarity into a more continuous spectrum, for it means that there is not just one axis on which the disciplines can be laid out. We need, rather, something like multidimensional graph paper in which all the complex parameters which describe the interconnections and contrasts can be plotted simultaneously. In these ways, further reflection on the nature of academic disciplines as well as developments within individual disciplines have made any binary division into *two* cultures look more implausible than ever. But there was a deeper, and in some ways more interesting, point embedded in Snow's analysis, namely, the cultural impact of the increasing specialisation of knowledge.

Specialisation

Outsiders tend to see uniformity in other groups and fine distinctions within their own. From the perspective of a biochemist or electrical engineer the differences between an empirical sociologist and a modern social historian may seem barely perceptible; similarly, to the classicist or the art historian what the different branches of physics share seems far more salient than what divides them. But all these fields or sub-fields have increasingly developed their own concerns, methods, and vocabularies to the point where no one division is obviously more significant than all others. The theoretical economist and the critic of French poetry are as mutually incomprehensible in their professional work as ever 'scientists' and 'humanists' were supposed to be.

It is fruitless to lament the process of specialisation as such: it is the precondition of intellectual progress, and often represents an impressive refinement of concepts and techniques. It makes no more sense to insist that every word written by the professional philosopher should be accessible to the uninstructed lay reader than it does to impose that standard on crystallographers. The interesting questions are, rather, about the ways in which such specialisms relate to the wider culture and the impact they have upon discussion of those matters which can never be reduced, without remainder, to the preserve of one academic discipline.

Here it may be helpful to emphasise another simple truth, namely that we do not have just *one* identity, we are not exhaustively defined by our professional training and occupation. We inhabit overlapping identities – social, racial, sexual, religious, intellectual, political – and no one of them alone is always domi-nant or consistently determines our responses. Thus, we do not participate in public affairs and public discussion primarily as organic chemists or social anthropologists, just as we may not read a new popular account of recent advances in astronomy or the latest biography of Elizabeth I primarily in our capacities as immunologists or macro-economists. One of the hazards of academic life is the way its ethos and organisa-tion encourages us to exaggerate the power and impor-tance of these disciplinary affiliations to the neglect of other, often deeper, ties and allegiances. There is, simi-larly, not just one form of a possible 'common culture'. Commonality takes various forms, and we need to think in terms of *degrees* of participation in these shared worlds rather than in terms of simple inclusion or exclusion.

When Snow sought to illustrate the alleged division between the cultures, he notoriously spoke of those in the humanities not knowing the Second Law of Thermodynamics.[41] Leaving aside the aptness or otherwise of this particular example, we may question whether it is most fruitful to think of a common culture so purely in terms of a shared body of *information*. Sharp limits are, anyway, set to that possibility from the moment at which choices between subjects need to be made in school or university education. But, more fundamentally, insofar as the cultural effects of specialisation are a matter for anxiety or regret (and perhaps all talk of 'two cultures' betrays a yearning that division should yield to unity), it is not because they are being judged against an ideal of everyone commanding the same body of knowledge, but rather because they threaten to make it impossible to sustain the kind of debate or mutually intelligible exchange of views upon which the effective conduct of a society's affairs depends.

This surely suggests that what is wanted is not to force potential physicists to read a bit of Dickens and potential literary critics to mug up some basic theorems. Rather, we need to encourage the growth of the intellectual equivalent of bilingualism, a capacity not only to exercise the language of our respective specialisms, but also to attend to, learn from, and eventually contribute to, wider cultural conversations. Obviously, it may

[41] So notorious did this example become that it even featured in a comic song by Flanders and Swan included in their collection *At The Drop of Another Hat*.

help if one's education has not been too specialised too early, and Snow's warning remains pertinent here. But more important still will be the nurturing *within* the ethos of the various academic specialisms not only of some understanding of how their activities fit into a larger cultural whole, but also of a recognition that attending to these larger questions is not some kind of off-duty voluntary work, but is an integral and properly rewarded part of professional achievement in the given field.

Clearly, it is not within the power of any one academic discipline to create this ethos unilaterally. Both the possibilities of communication and the distribution of esteem depend on favourable cultural traditions; differing attitudes towards intellectuals in France and in Britain, for example, confer a different standing upon participation by academics in public debate, and this in turn gets internalised as part of the process of professional formation. In general, the pressures of competitive research, especially in the natural sciences, tend to relegate engagement with larger cultural or ethical questions to the status of soft options, to be pursued only by those not able to maintain the pace at the cutting edge of research. But there are numerous occasions when specialists, whether in natural science or anything else, have to put the case for their enterprise in language non-specialists can understand. This holds for activites as different as speaking at a university committee or reviewing a book in a national newspaper – or, to take an example close to Snow's heart, advising a government department on the use of a particular form of technology. One encouraging sign here, amidst a general hardening of specialist identities, is the way a few brilliant individuals like Stephen Jay Gould,

Richard Dawkins, or Stephen Hawking have illustrated the possibility of combining creative scientific work at the highest level with communication with a wider audience. And this has been achieved, it should be noted, not by any one of these individuals attempting to be a modern Leonardo, commanding advanced knowledge in widely disparate fields, but rather by retaining or acquiring the skill, and the desire, to impart to a non-specialist readership some sense of the significance if not the detail of extremely technical research.

One of the axes along which disciplines can be classified assumes a particular prominence at this point. Different disciplines stand in revealingly different relations to the activity of writing. In many forms of experimental science, writing plays no really creative role: it is not itself a process of discovery, as it is in the humanities, but an after-the-event report – 'writing up', as the idiom revealingly has it. Accuracy, clarity, economy are certainly required in the presentation of results, but arranging one's findings in intelligible form is regarded by many research scientists as something of a chore. When scientists admire the 'elegance' of a theory or finding – and it is worth remembering that they do so frequently – it is usually its conceptual or mathematical neatness or the economy of its explanatory principles they are admiring. Elegance of style tends not to be cultivated or prized as a professional ideal, though individual scientists may cherish it. But in many humanities subjects, not only may the most creative thinking be done in the very process of writing, but the manner in which a book or article is written is *itself* the chief embodiment of the level of understanding that has been reached. In this respect, work in the humanities tends to be both more individual and less susceptible of paraphrase or synthetic re-statement. Correspondingly, introductory teaching in the literary subjects tends to use anthologies rather than text-books; the original form of expression is not dispensable.

This difference then feeds back into the earlier point about the ways in which the research practices and ideals of particular disciplines may discourage the development of those aptitudes and inclinations required by participation in public debate. And this is not just a matter of literacy in any narrow sense. Since Snow, the tendency has been to deplore the 'scientific illiteracy' of public figures and scholars in the humanities alike, but at least as damaging can be the historical and philosophical illiteracy of research scientists. Moreover, it is far from obvious that either administrators or the general public have any greater appreciation of the real nature of the intellectual activities pursued in the humanities than in the sciences. Indeed, in some ways the utilitarian public language of modern liberal democracies, which is intensely suspicious of non-demonstrable judgements of quality and intolerant of non-quantifiable assertions of value, makes it easier to justify fundamental research in the natural sciences, with its promise of medical, industrial, and similar applications, than to justify what is anyway only with some awkwardness called 'research' in the humanities. In this respect, the specialist's disdain for communicating with a wider audience may, as we move into the twenty-first century, have more practically damaging consequences for the well-being of the humanities than of the sciences.

For all its defects, Snow's argument has the valuable effect of preventing us from being complacent about the condition of knowledge in our time. The rigid divisions between disciplines, the lack of mutual comprehension, the misplaced feelings of superiority or disdain in different professional groups – these should be seen as *problems*, not fatalistically accepted as part of the immutable order of things (or, to quote Wolf Lepenies once more: 'What we need is less tragic self-conceit and rigidity of principle and more irony, self-criticism and the ability to see our own scientific work as though from the outside'[42]). But Snow also linked this topic to some larger issues of immense consequence for the future of the planet, and we now need to consider how well his argument on these matters has stood the test of time.

The 'two cultures' in a changing world

One of the most familiar tropes of modernity is the bemused reflection that in one's own lifetime the pace of change has accelerated to the point where it almost escapes comprehension, and we must beware the inducements to cultural pessimism offered by those who lament that the process has got out of control (when was it ever 'under control'?). Rather than taking for granted that anything diagnosed as a problem in 1959 can only have worsened in the intervening decades, it may be helpful to consider some of the ways in which the bearing of Snow's 'two cultures' thesis needs to be modified in the light of changes which are neither wholly beneficial nor wholly disastrous. For example, the educated public's exposure to science and to the impact of scientific advance has increased enormously during this period. There has probably been no greater single force for diffusing an interest in and understanding of the work of scientists than television.

[42] Lepenies, 'Direction of the Disciplines', 64.

It is understandable that the role of television should hardly have figured in Snow's thinking, since he was speaking just at the beginning of the period of widespread TV ownership in Britain (and anyway, as we have seen, the main outlines of his position were set in the 1930s). But television has not only spread a great deal of scientific information, albeit in simplified form; it has also stirred the imagination about the mysteries of the natural world in millions of those whose formal education failed to leave them with any sense of the nature of excitement of scientific enquiry.

Furthermore, the micro-electronic revolution which has taken place since Snow was writing is having as great an impact on daily life as the invention of the railway or the internal combustion engine had on that of earlier generations, and the rapidity of the technical advances continually threatens to defy ordinary understanding.[43] Even the ancient task of trying to give thought the form of prose has been more deeply affected by this development than by any change since the invention of printing – a sentence which has itself been created and revised by tapping on a set of little plastic squares connected by a cable to a hole in the wall. Computers are only the most impressive of the host of machines which are becoming standard features of daily life and which provide their users with some rudimentary experience of the power of applied science.

[43] For example, at present microprocessor performance doubles every two years; memory devices quadruple in size every three years: 'in 1980 the processor could execute about 39,000 instructions while you typed a character, in 1990 about 1,250,000 . . . If we scale up to a comprehensible one second the time for a processor to execute one instruction, then in 1980 humans typed at a rate of about two characters per day, in 1990 at about a character a fortnight.' Jean Bacon, 'Computer Science and Computer Education', *The Cambridge Review*, 112 (1991), 174.

Perhaps a particularly ostentatious form of bad faith is required of any latter-day 'literary intellectual' who composes on a word processor and then faxes to a journal a jeremiad about the wholly negative effects of scientific advance.

But although such changes may have produced a greater appreciation of the centrality of science in the modern world, by their very success they inevitably engender ambivalent responses. There is surely less snobbish disdain for science as something meanly utilitarian and grubby than Snow thought he detected (perhaps reflecting his own social experience before the war), but there would appear to be even more anxiety about its potentially harmful consequences. The whole question of human treatment of the natural world exemplifies the dialectic by which the extension of scientific control and an increasing anxiety about its effects are tied to each other. What gets forgotten in the more sweeping and alarmist complaints about technology's harmful impact on the environment is the fact that it is precisely further scientific advances that have enabled us to identify and analyse many of these effects (the hole in the ozone layer provides one obvious example here). The more positive, and realistic, response to such problems is surely to recognise that the capacities that have produced threatening technologies are also our best hope of producing benign ones. Similarly, Snow feared that an inadequate level of scientific education had led to science being undervalued, but a period which has seen an enormous expansion of scientific education across the world has, hardly surprisingly, been accompanied by an unease lest science and scientific reasoning become overvalued. Inevitably, these reactions sometimes take the extreme form of urging mankind to repudiate the spiritually and ecologically devastating enterprise of science altogether.[44] But there is an element of moral posturing as well as a lack of realism in such reactions, and again the more constructive response is surely to seek to build into scientific education itself an awareness of the limits and dangers, as well as of the immense benefits, of our increased knowledge of the natural world.

Education was, of course, seen to be the root of the problem Snow had diagnosed, though it is sometimes forgotten that, apart from urging Britain to turn out a greater number of trained scientists, he did not really put forward any specific educational proposals. As I have already remarked, he was writing at a time when the last years of school education in England were particularly specialised, and this clearly influenced his analysis. No other major educational system allowed quite so much specialisation so early. But even in England in recent decades there have been attempts (not always successful, it must be said) to expand the range of subjects studied in school and university, and elsewhere the trend appears to be to maintain children's exposure to a balance of subjects till as late as possible. More than twenty years ago, George Steiner (himself a notable exception to patterns of early specialisation, having majored in physics before going on to become a leading literary critic) warned that in the future those with only the old verbal skills could be in danger of becoming 'word-helots', excluded from the advanced processes of their society,[45] but it would seem

[44] Davies and Gribbin speak of 'the current anti-science backlash in Western society' (*The Matter Myth*, p. 20); a widely discussed recent example of this reaction is Bryan Appleyard, *Understanding the Present* (London, 1992).

[45] George Steiner, *In Bluebeard's Castle: Some Notes Towards the Re-definition of Culture* (London, 1971), p. 100. Steiner was

that the need for basic mathematical as well as verbal literacy is being increasingly acknowledged, even if as yet imperfectly implemented.

It is fatally easy, in discussing this theme, to slip into dealing with 'science' and 'literature' as stable entities, frozen at one moment in time (usually the moment when our own views were first formed). When Snow spoke of 'science' he tended to have in mind the kind of thing that went on in the Cavendish Laboratory in Cambridge, but, quite apart from the intellectual changes mentioned in the previous section, there is a danger of parochialism here. Taking 'scientific research' in its broadest sense, one has to acknowledge a preponderant American presence: in 1984 one commentator calculated that 'half of the Western world's research and development is carried out in the United States which . . . spends more money on science than Japan and the industrialised nations of Europe combined'. Furthermore, an increasing proportion of this 'research' (much of which, of course, is not basic science) is carried on in laboratories funded directly or indirectly by private industry, and even where this is not apparent we need to recognise 'the dominant role of the private sector in setting the agenda for the public funding of science'.[46] In practice, much of what is commonly regarded as 'science' has to be understood at the end of the twentieth century less as disinterested enquiry and more as part of the commercial strategies of drug

sympathetic to the spirit of Snow's thesis, and endorsed the view that the essential difference of sensibility between scientists and 'humanists' lay in their respective orientation to the future and the past. See also his contribution to a symposium on 'The Two Cultures Re-visited', *The Cambridge Review*, 108 (1987), 13–14.

[46] David Dickson, *The New Politics of Science* (Chicago, 1984; rev. edn 1989), pp. 4, 44.

companies, aerospace industries, and the like. Similarly, there would be another kind of parochialism in freezing 'English literature' around the canon acknowledged in the mid-twentieth century. In the last three decades, the publication and international success of non-British literature in English has expanded enormously. 'English literature' is now only one of the literatures in English, the one with the longest and richest history perhaps, but a minor presence in the contemporary world and not obviously destined to be the most creative or significant in the next century. Instead of Snow's research physicist and literary critic encountering mutual incomprehension over the Second Law of Thermodynamics and the plays of Shakespeare at a Cambridge High Table, the emblematic figures representing the relations between his 'two cultures' at the end of the twentieth century should perhaps be a Singapore-Chinese economic analyst E-mailing her American software-designer boyfriend about the latest Afro-Caribbean poet to win the Nobel Prize for literature.

As this should remind us, one of the other changes that has been happening at an accelerating pace since Snow's time has been the spread of English as an international language. Snow emphasised the gulfs separating national cultures as well as intellectual cultures, but both his contrasts have perhaps been a little softened by the way in which an increasing proportion of human communication is carried on in that special dialect, or cluster of dialects, known as 'English as a second language'. The commercial and technological forces driving this development are hardly likely to diminish – we are all, as it were, air-traffic controllers now. Partly for these reasons, the *content* of education in different countries, especially the less 'developed', displays an increasing convergence. Above all, the dominance of a kind of English as the required medium for serious science is nearly complete: when in 1989 even the *Annales de l'Institut Pasteur* in Paris, one of the premier scientific publications in the country that has been most conscious of the distinctive grandeur and historic status of its own language, changed its name to *Research in Microbiology* and went over to wholly English-language articles, a telling symbolic step had been taken towards the world scientific community becoming ever more of a 'global village'.

Snow later reflected that in some ways he wished he had stuck to his original intention to title his lecture 'The Rich and the Poor' since this 'was what I intended to be the centre of the whole argument' (p.79 below). His sense that this was the dominant issue facing the world and that a recognition of the 'remediable suffering of most of [our] fellow humans' brought with it 'responsibilities which, once they are seen, cannot be denied' remains the most admirable and persuasive feature of his lecture. But it now seems harder to share the somewhat blithe confidence with which Snow spoke of how 'backward' countries needed 'modernisation'. He was, of course, far from alone in speaking in this way at the time: indeed, in the 1950s and early 1960s there flourished, especially in the United States, a whole sub-field of social science known as 'modernisation theory', which rested on the social evolutionist assumption that all societies were progressing along essentially the same track but at very different speeds. Seen thus, the task was to accelerate the development in 'backward' societies of recognisably 'modern' social structures such as small family units, of cultural attitudes such as secular individualism, and of political arrangements such as representative democracy, and so on.

Snow evidently believed that industrialisation would bring the other desired characteristics in its train, that an understanding of the application of new technology was the central requirement among those attempting to aid the process, and that a lack of scientific education among the administrative elites of the advanced societies was the chief obstacle. The experience of various parts of the developing world in the last three decades has cast doubt on each of these assumptions. Social practices and cultural attitudes have proved remarkably intractable and have not followed the approved evolutionary course; introducing forms of technology derived from or adapted to local conditions has often yielded better results than the wholesale importation of Western methods; the political barriers to successful exploitation of resources have proved far greater than was anticipated; and so on. But in 1959 Snow was briskly confident: 'For the task of totally industrialising a major country . . . it only takes will to train enough scientists and engineers and technicians . . . Tradition and technical background seem to count for surprisingly little' (p. 45 below). In practice, cultural and political traditions seem to have proved a good deal more important than this, whether positively, as in the economic development of East Asia, or negatively, as in sub-Saharan Africa.

The continuing purchase of Snow's case has been weakened by these developments in at least one important respect. For him, the most telling practical consequence of the divide between the two cultures lay in the way in which the traditional cultural epitomised by the 'literary intellectuals' scorned the economic and social benefits that would flow from the export of technology to the 'backward' countries. It is arguable that such attitudes were in fact neither so widespread nor so politically effective as he seemed to assume; there is no evidence that decisions made in the higher reaches of the British Civil Service, for example, reflected the 'Luddite' attitudes he detected in the likes of D.H. Lawrence or Wyndham Lewis. But beyond that, the experience of recent decades has suggested that improving the standards of living in Third World countries rests more on understanding the very complex operation of political and cultural forces at work than on understanding the science involved in the latest technological advance. In addition, the setting in which governments operate has changed, as the decisions of multi-national companies and financial institutions play a greater part in determining the prosperity of the poorer parts of the world. Here, too, the assertion of effective political control over these forces has come to seem more important than any of the purely technocratic questions involved. More broadly still, Snow reflected some of the confidence of the 'end of ideology' era that politics would become more and more pragmatic and less and less driven by conflicting ideologies. While in one respect the end of the Cold War may seem to confirm part of this prognosis, in practice the world appears more rather than less riven by such 'unmodern' urges as nationalism, ethnic loyalty, and religious fundamentalism. Not only are these forces not obviously susceptible to being tamed or eliminated by economic and technological improvement, but also they are the kinds of phenomena which are most resistant to being understood in terms derived from or modelled on the natural sciences. In all these ways, therefore, it has not become more obvious since

lxix

Snow wrote that, to put it in provokingly stark terms, an education in physics or chemistry is a better preparation for handling the world's problems than an education in history or philosophy.

It is evident from Snow's public pronouncements as well as from his novels that he was ultimately less interested in public debate than in what happens behind closed doors: his assumed model of how the 'two cultures' thesis bore upon policy-making consisted of a small group of politicians and their advisers.[47] The political experience of the last three decades has emphasised the drawbacks rather than the benefits of 'behind closed doors' politics, and pointed to the need, in the face of huge practical and social difficulties, of sustaining some kind of public debate on the major issues requiring decision. No one can reasonably deny the value, and for some purposes the necessity, of basic numeracy and scientific literacy; but ideas operate in particular historical settings, and in the major industrial countries at the end of the twentieth century an insistence on the overriding need for greater scientific and mathematical competence can be two-edged and even dangerous. It may be far more damaging to encourage, however inadvertently, the reduction of the processes of decision-making to matters that can be counted or measured than it would be to appear complacent about an inadequate level of technological or statistical understanding. At least as pressing as the need for a basic scientific literacy is the need to develop and diffuse a

[47] His 'Science and Government', in particular, illustrates his fascination with this theme, as well as suggesting his own desire to be privy to discussions at the highest level. All the pieces collected in *Public Affairs* reflect the tone of this wholly male world of briskly competent meritocrats, conscious of access to power and flushed with a pride in their own shrewdness.

public language in which non-quantifiable considerations can be given their proper weight.

But perhaps Snow himself should have the last word. In 1971 he acknowledged that he had 'remained dissatisfied with the purely academic formulation of "The Two Cultures" concept', and that he had tried on several occasions to refine the claim.[48] But the larger global issues underlying his case had only come to seem to him more central and more urgent, and he returned to them in his last major public statement, 'The State of Siege', delivered as an address at, appropriately enough, the same place (Fulton, Missouri) as Winston Churchill had made his famous 'iron curtain' speech. 'One hears young people asking for a cause', Snow observed.[49] He offered to give an answer in the simplest terms, and he emphasised that he had intended his idea of 'the two cultures' to help contribute to the realisation of these goals. 'Peace. Food. No more people than the earth can take. That is the cause.'

[48] *Public Affairs*, p. 11.
[49] 'The State of Siege' (1968), *Public Affairs*, p.220.

A NOTE ON FURTHER READING

For a complete and annotated guide both to Snow's own works and to writing about him up until 1980, see Paul Boytinck, *C.P. Snow: A Reference Guide* (Boston, 1980). Most of Snow's novels are still in print; the eleven-volume *Strangers and Brothers* sequence was reissued in a three-volume omnibus edition (London, 1972). His major lectures and essays are collected in *Public Affairs* (London, 1971); his essay-portraits of prominent figures are collected in *Variety of Men* (London, 1967), and *The Physicists* (London, 1981).

The fullest biographical source is Philip Snow, *Stranger and Brother: A Portrait of C.P. Snow* (London, 1982). Some additional material may be gleaned from John Halperin, *C.P. Snow: An Oral Biography* (Brighton, 1983). There are several critical studies of Snow's fiction, including David Shusterman, *C.P. Snow* (Boston, 1975) in the 'Twayne's English Authors' series. The most recent general study (which I have been unable to consult) is John de la Mothe, *C.P. Snow and the Struggle of Modernity* (Austin, 1992). F.R. Leavis's *Two Cultures? The Significance of C.P. Snow* (London, 1962) is reprinted in his *Nor Shall My Sword: Discourses on Pluralism, Compassion and Social Hope* (London, 1972); the best recent study of his work is Michael Bell, *F.R. Leavis* (London, 1988). There is a vast literature on the 'two cultures' theme, most of it dating from the 1960s: for representative samples, see David K. Cornelius and Edwin St Vincent (eds.), *Cultures in Conflict: Perspectives* on the Snow–Leavis Controversy (Chicago, 1964), and William H. Davenport *The One Culture* (New York, 1970).

PREFACE TO
· THE SECOND EDITION

Since the original lecture has been written about a good deal, I have thought it best to leave it as it was first printed, apart from the correction of two small inaccuracies.

In the second part, as I explain, I have looked at the lecture again in the light of various comments and the passage of four years.

23 September 1963   C.P.S.

I. THE REDE LECTURE, 1959

I

THE TWO CULTURES

IT is about three years since I made a sketch in print
of a problem which had been on my mind for some
time.[1] It was a problem I could not avoid just
because of the circumstances of my life. The only
credentials I had to ruminate on the subject at all came
through those circumstances, through nothing more
than a set of chances. Anyone with similar experience
would have seen much the same things and I think
made very much the same comments about them. It
just happened to be an unusual experience. By training
I was a scientist: by vocation I was a writer. That was
all. It was a piece of luck, if you like, that arose through
coming from a poor home.

But my personal history isn't the point now. All
that I need say is that I came to Cambridge and did a
bit of research here at a time of major scientific activity.
I was privileged to have a ringside view of one of the
most wonderful creative periods in all physics. And it
happened through the flukes of war—including meet-
ing W. L. Bragg in the buffet on Kettering station on a
very cold morning in 1939, which had a determining
influence on my practical life—that I was able, and

indeed morally forced, to keep that ringside view ever since. So for thirty years I have had to be in touch with scientists not only out of curiosity, but as part of a working existence. During the same thirty years I was trying to shape the books I wanted to write, which in due course took me among writers.

There have been plenty of days when I have spent the working hours with scientists and then gone off at night with some literary colleagues. I mean that literally. I have had, of course, intimate friends among both scientists and writers. It was through living among these groups and much more, I think, through moving regularly from one to the other and back again that I got occupied with the problem of what, long before I put it on paper, I christened to myself as the 'two cultures'. For constantly I felt I was moving among two groups—comparable in intelligence, identical in race, not grossly different in social origin, earning about the same incomes, who had almost ceased to communicate at all, who in intellectual, moral and psychological climate had so little in common that instead of going from Burlington House or South Kensington to Chelsea, one might have crossed an ocean.

In fact, one had travelled much further than across an ocean—because after a few thousand Atlantic miles, one found Greenwich Village talking precisely the same language as Chelsea, and both having about as much communication with M.I.T. as though the scientists spoke nothing but Tibetan. For this is not just our problem; owing to some of our educational and social idiosyncrasies, it is slightly exaggerated here, owing to another English social peculiarity it is slightly minimised; by and large this is a problem of the entire West.

By this I intend something serious. I am not thinking of the pleasant story of how one of the more convivial Oxford greats dons—I have heard the story attributed to A. L. Smith—came over to Cambridge to dine. The date is perhaps the 1890's. I think it must have been at St John's, or possibly Trinity. Anyway, Smith was sitting at the right hand of the President—or Vice-Master—and he was a man who liked to include all round him in the conversation, although he was not immediately encouraged by the expressions of his neighbours. He addressed some cheerful Oxonian chit-chat at the one opposite to him, and got a grunt. He then tried the man on his own right hand and got another grunt. Then, rather to his surprise, one looked at the other and said, 'Do you know what he's talking about?' 'I haven't the least idea.' At this, even Smith was getting out of his depth. But the President, acting as a social emollient, put him at his ease by saying, 'Oh, those are mathematicians! We never talk to *them.*'

No, I intend something serious. I believe the intellectual life of the whole of western society is increasingly being split into two polar groups. When I say the intellectual life, I mean to include also a large part of our practical life, because I should be the last person to

3

suggest the two can at the deepest level be distinguished. I shall come back to the practical life a little later. Two polar groups: at one pole we have the literary intellectuals, who incidentally while no one was looking took to referring to themselves as 'intellectuals' as though there were no others. I remember G. H. Hardy once remarking to me in mild puzzlement, some time in the 1930's: 'Have you noticed how the word "intellectual" is used nowadays? There seems to be a new definition which certainly doesn't include Rutherford or Eddington or Dirac or Adrian or me. It does seem rather odd, don't y' know.'[2]

Literary intellectuals at one pole—at the other scientists, and as the most representative, the physical scientists. Between the two a gulf of mutual incomprehension—sometimes (particularly among the young) hostility and dislike, but most of all lack of understanding. They have a curious distorted image of each other. Their attitudes are so different that, even on the level of emotion, they can't find much common ground. Non-scientists tend to think of scientists as brash and boastful. They hear Mr T. S. Eliot, who just for these illustrations we can take as an archetypal figure, saying about his attempts to revive verse-drama that we can hope for very little, but that he would feel content if he and his co-workers could prepare the ground for a new Kyd or a new Greene. That is the tone, restricted and constrained, with which literary intellectuals are at home: it is the subdued voice of their culture. Then they hear a much louder voice, that of another archetypal figure, Rutherford, trumpeting: 'This is the heroic age of science! This is the Elizabethan age!' Many of us heard that, and a good many other statements beside which that was mild; and we weren't left in any doubt whom Rutherford was casting for the role of Shakespeare. What is hard for the literary intellectuals to understand, imaginatively or intellectually, is that he was absolutely right.

And compare 'this is the way the world ends, not with a bang but a whimper'—incidentally, one of the least likely scientific prophecies ever made—compare that with Rutherford's famous repartee, 'Lucky fellow, Rutherford, always on the crest of the wave.' 'Well, I made the wave, didn't I?'

The non-scientists have a rooted impression that the scientists are shallowly optimistic, unaware of man's condition. On the other hand, the scientists believe that the literary intellectuals are totally lacking in foresight, peculiarly unconcerned with their brother men, in a deep sense anti-intellectual, anxious to restrict both art and thought to the existential moment. And so on. Anyone with a mild talent for invective could produce plenty of this kind of subterranean back-chat. On each side there is some of it which is not entirely baseless. It is all destructive. Much of it rests on misinterpretations which are dangerous. I should like to deal with two of the most profound of these now, one on each side.

First, about the scientists' optimism. This is an accusation which has been made so often that it has become a platitude. It has been made by some of the acutest non-scientific minds of the day. But it depends upon a confusion between the individual experience and the social experience, between the individual condition of man and his social condition. Most of the scientists I have known well have felt—just as deeply as the non-scientists I have known well—that the individual condition of each of us is tragic. Each of us is alone: sometimes we escape from solitariness, through love or affection or perhaps creative moments, but those triumphs of life are pools of light we make for ourselves while the edge of the road is black: each of us dies alone. Some scientists I have known have had faith in revealed religion. Perhaps with them the sense of the tragic condition is not so strong. I don't know. With most people of deep feeling, however high-spirited and happy they are, sometimes most with those who are happiest and most high-spirited, it seems to be right in the fibres, part of the weight of life. That is as true of the scientists I have known best as of anyone at all.

But nearly all of them—and this is where the colour of hope genuinely comes in—would see no reason why, just because the individual condition is tragic, so must the social condition be. Each of us is solitary: each of us dies alone: all right, that's a fate against which we can't struggle—but there is plenty in our condition which is not fate, and against which we are less than human unless we do struggle.

Most of our fellow human beings, for instance, are

underfed and die before their time. In the crudest terms, *that* is the social condition. There is a moral trap which comes through the insight into man's loneliness: it tempts one to sit back, complacent in one's unique tragedy, and let the others go without a meal.

As a group, the scientists fall into that trap less than others. They are inclined to be impatient to see if something can be done: and inclined to think that it can be done, until it's proved otherwise. That is their real optimism, and it's an optimism that the rest of us badly need.

In reverse, the same spirit, tough and good and determined to fight it out at the side of their brother men, has made scientists regard the other culture's social attitudes as contemptible. That is too facile: some of them are, but they are a temporary phase and not to be taken as representative.

I remember being cross-examined by a scientist of distinction. 'Why do most writers take on social opinions which would have been thought distinctly uncivilised and démodé at the time of the Plantagenets? Wasn't that true of most of the famous twentieth-century writers? Yeats, Pound, Wyndham Lewis, nine out of ten of those who have dominated literary sensibility in our time—weren't they not only politically silly, but politically wicked? Didn't the influence of all they represent bring Auschwitz that much nearer?'

I thought at the time, and I still think, that the correct answer was not to defend the indefensible. It was no use saying that Yeats, according to friends whose judgment I trust, was a man of singular magnanimity of character, as well as a great poet. It was no use denying the facts, which are broadly true. The honest answer was that there is, in fact, a connection, which literary persons were culpably slow to see, between some kinds of early twentieth-century art and the most imbecile expressions of anti-social feeling.[3] That was one reason, among many, why some of us turned our backs on the art and tried to hack out a new or different way for ourselves.[4]

But though many of those writers dominated literary sensibility for a generation, that is no longer so, or at least to nothing like the same extent. Literature changes more slowly than science. It hasn't the same automatic corrective, and so its misguided periods are longer. But it is ill-considered of scientists to judge writers on the evidence of the period 1914–50.

Those are two of the misunderstandings between the two cultures. I should say, since I began to talk about them—the two cultures, that is—I have had some criticism. Most of my scientific acquaintances think that there is something in it, and so do most of the practising artists I know. But I have been argued with by non-scientists of strong down-to-earth interests. Their view is that it is an over-simplification, and that if one is going to talk in these terms there ought to be at least three cultures. They argue that, though they are not scientists themselves, they would share a good deal of the scientific feeling. They would have as little

8

use—perhaps, since they knew more about it, even less use—for the recent literary culture as the scientists themselves. J. H. Plumb, Alan Bullock and some of my American sociological friends have said that they vigorously refuse to be corralled in a cultural box with people they wouldn't be seen dead with, or to be regarded as helping to produce a climate which would not permit of social hope.

I respect those arguments. The number 2 is a very dangerous number: that is why the dialectic is a dangerous process. Attempts to divide anything into two ought to be regarded with much suspicion. I have thought a long time about going in for further refinements: but in the end I have decided against. I was searching for something a little more than a dashing metaphor, a good deal less than a cultural map: and for those purposes the two cultures is about right, and subtilising any more would bring more disadvantages than it's worth.

At one pole, the scientific culture really is a culture, not only in an intellectual but also in an anthropological sense. That is, its members need not, and of course often do not, always completely understand each other; biologists more often than not will have a pretty hazy idea of contemporary physics; but there are common attitudes, common standards and patterns of behaviour, common approaches and assumptions. This goes surprisingly wide and deep. It cuts across other mental patterns, such as those of religion or politics or class.

Statistically, I suppose slightly more scientists are in

9

religious terms unbelievers, compared with the rest of the intellectual world—though there are plenty who are religious, and that seems to be increasingly so among the young. Statistically also, slightly more scientists are on the Left in open politics—though again, plenty always have called themselves conservatives, and that also seems to be more common among the young. Compared with the rest of the intellectual world, considerably more scientists in this country and probably in the U.S. come from poor families.[5] Yet over a whole range of thought and behaviour, none of that matters very much. In their working, and in much of their emotional life, their attitudes are closer to other scientists than to non-scientists who in religion or politics or class have the same labels as themselves. If I were to risk a piece of shorthand, I should say that naturally they had the future in their bones.

They may or may not like it, but they have it. That was as true of the conservatives J. J. Thomson and Lindemann as of the radicals Einstein or Blackett: as true of the Christian A. H. Compton as of the materialist Bernal: of the aristocrats de Broglie or Russell as of the proletarian Faraday: of those born rich, like Thomas Merton or Victor Rothschild, as of Rutherford, who was the son of an odd-job handyman. Without thinking about it, they respond alike. That is what a culture means.

At the other pole, the spread of attitudes is wider. It is obvious that between the two, as one moves through intellectual society from the physicists to the literary intellectuals, there are all kinds of tones of feeling on the way. But I believe the pole of total incomprehension of science radiates its influence on all the rest. That total incomprehension gives, much more pervasively than we realise, living in it, an unscientific flavour to the whole 'traditional' culture, and that unscientific flavour is often, much more than we admit, on the point of turning anti-scientific. The feelings of one pole become the anti-feelings of the other. If the scientists have the future in their bones, then the traditional culture responds by wishing the future did not exist.[6] It is the traditional culture, to an extent remarkably little diminished by the emergence of the scientific one, which manages the western world.

This polarisation is sheer loss to us all. To us as people, and to our society. It is at the same time practical and intellectual and creative loss, and I repeat that it is false to imagine that those three considerations are clearly separable. But for a moment I want to concentrate on the intellectual loss.

The degree of incomprehension on both sides is the kind of joke which has gone sour. There are about fifty thousand working scientists in the country and about eighty thousand professional engineers or applied scientists. During the war and in the years since, my colleagues and I have had to interview somewhere between thirty to forty thousand of these—that is, about 25 per cent. The number is large enough to give us a fair sample, though of the men we talked to most would still be under forty. We were able to find out a certain amount of what they read and thought about. I confess that even I, who am fond of them and respect them, was a bit shaken. We hadn't quite expected that the links with the traditional culture should be so tenuous, nothing more than a formal touch of the cap.

As one would expect, some of the very best scientists had and have plenty of energy and interest to spare, and we came across several who had read everything that literary people talk about. But that's very rare. Most of the rest, when one tried to probe for what books they had read, would modestly confess, 'Well, I've *tried* a bit of Dickens', rather as though Dickens were an extraordinarily esoteric, tangled and dubiously rewarding writer, something like Rainer Maria Rilke. In fact that is exactly how they do regard him: we thought that discovery, that Dickens had been transformed into the type-specimen of literary incomprehensibility, was one of the oddest results of the whole exercise.

But of course, in reading him, in reading almost any writer whom we should value, they are just touching their caps to the traditional culture. They have their own culture, intensive, rigorous, and constantly in action. This culture contains a great deal of argument, usually much more rigorous, and almost always at a higher conceptual level, than literary persons' arguments—even though the scientists do cheerfully use words in senses which literary persons don't recognise, the senses are exact ones, and when they talk about 'subjective', 'objective', 'philosophy' or 'progressive',[7] they know what they mean, even though it isn't what one is accustomed to expect.

Remember, these are very intelligent men. Their culture is in many ways an exacting and admirable one. It doesn't contain much art, with the exception, an important exception, of music. Verbal exchange, insistent argument. Long-playing records. Colour-photography. The ear, to some extent the eye. Books, very little, though perhaps not many would go so far as one hero, who perhaps I should admit was further down the scientific ladder than the people I've been talking about—who, when asked what books he read, replied firmly and confidently: 'Books? I prefer to use my books as tools.' It was very hard not to let the mind wander—what sort of tool would a book make? Perhaps a hammer? A primitive digging instrument?

Of books, though, very little. And of the books which to most literary persons are bread and butter, novels, history, poetry, plays, almost nothing at all. It isn't that they're not interested in the psychological or moral or social life. In the social life, they certainly are, more than most of us. In the moral, they are by and large the soundest group of intellectuals we have; there is a moral component right in the grain of science itself, and almost all scientists form their own judgments of the moral life. In the psychological they have as much interest as most of us, though occasionally I fancy they come to it rather late. It isn't that they lack the interests. It is much more that the whole literature of the traditional culture doesn't seem to them relevant to those interests. They are, of course, dead wrong. As a result, their imaginative understanding is less than it could be. They are self-impoverished.

But what about the other side? They are impoverished too—perhaps more seriously, because they are vainer about it. They still like to pretend that the traditional culture is the whole of 'culture', as though the natural order didn't exist. As though the exploration of the natural order was of no interest either in its own value or its consequences. As though the scientific edifice of the physical world was not, in its intellectual depth, complexity and articulation, the most beautiful and wonderful collective work of the mind of man. Yet most non-scientists have no conception of that edifice at all. Even if they want to have it, they can't. It is rather as though, over an immense range of intellectual experience, a whole group was tone-deaf. Except that this tone-deafness doesn't come by nature, but by training, or rather the absence of training.

As with the tone-deaf, they don't know what they miss. They give a pitying chuckle at the news of scientists who have never read a major work of English literature. They dismiss them as ignorant specialists. Yet their own ignorance and their own specialisation is just as startling. A good many times I have been present at gatherings of people who, by the standards of the traditional culture, are thought highly educated and who have with considerable gusto been expressing their incredulity at the illiteracy of scientists. Once or twice I have been provoked and have asked the company how many of them could describe the Second Law of Thermodynamics. The response was cold: it was also negative. Yet I was asking something which is about the scientific equivalent of: *Have you read a work of Shakespeare's?*

I now believe that if I had asked an even simpler question—such as, What do you mean by mass, or acceleration, which is the scientific equivalent of saying, *Can you read?*—not more than one in ten of the highly educated would have felt that I was speaking the same language. So the great edifice of modern physics goes up, and the majority of the cleverest people in the western world have about as much insight into it as their neolithic ancestors would have had.

Just one more of those questions, that my non-scientific friends regard as being in the worst of taste. Cambridge is a university where scientists and non-scientists meet every night at dinner.[8] About two years ago, one of the most astonishing discoveries in the whole history of science was brought off. I don't mean the sputnik—that was admirable for quite different reasons, as a feat of organisation and a triumphant use of existing knowledge. No, I mean the discovery at Columbia by Yang and Lee. It is a piece of work of the greatest beauty and originality, but the result is so startling that one forgets how beautiful the thinking is. It makes us think again about some of the fundamentals of the physical world. Intuition, common sense—they are neatly stood on their heads. The result is usually known as the non-conservation of parity. If there were any serious communication between the two cultures, this experiment would have been talked about at every High Table in Cambridge. Was it? I wasn't here: but I should like to ask the question.

There seems then to be no place where the cultures meet. I am not going to waste time saying that this is a pity. It is much worse than that. Soon I shall come to some practical consequences. But at the heart of thought and creation we are letting some of our best chances go by default. The clashing point of two subjects, two disciplines, two cultures—of two galaxies, so far as that goes—ought to produce creative chances. In the history of mental activity that has been where some of the break-throughs came. The chances are there now. But they are there, as it were, in a vacuum, because those in the two cultures can't talk to each other. It is bizarre how very little of twentieth-century science has been assimilated into twentieth-century art. Now and then one used to find poets conscientiously using scientific expressions, and getting them wrong—there was a time when 'refraction' kept cropping up in verse in a mystifying fashion, and when 'polarised light' was used as though writers were under the illusion that it was a specially admirable kind of light.

Of course, that isn't the way that science could be any good to art. It has got to be assimilated along with, and as part and parcel of, the whole of our mental experience, and used as naturally as the rest.

I said earlier that this cultural divide is not just an

English phenomenon: it exists all over the western world. But it probably seems at its sharpest in England, for two reasons. One is our fanatical belief in educational specialisation, which is much more deeply ingrained in us than in any country in the world, west or east. The other is our tendency to let our social forms crystallise. This tendency appears to get stronger, not weaker, the more we iron out economic inequalities: and this is specially true in education. It means that once anything like a cultural divide gets established, all the social forces operate to make it not less rigid, but more so.

The two cultures were already dangerously separate sixty years ago; but a prime minister like Lord Salisbury could have his own laboratory at Hatfield, and Arthur Balfour had a somewhat more than amateur interest in natural science. John Anderson did some research in inorganic chemistry in Leipzig before passing first into the Civil Service, and incidentally took a spread of subjects which is now impossible.[9] None of that degree of interchange at the top of the Establishment is likely, or indeed thinkable, now.[10]

In fact, the separation between the scientists and non-scientists is much less bridgeable among the young than it was even thirty years ago. Thirty years ago the cultures had long ceased to speak to each other: but at least they managed a kind of frozen smile across the gulf. Now the politeness has gone, and they just make faces. It is not only that the young scientists now feel that they are part of a culture on the rise while the other is in retreat. It is also, to be brutal, that the young scientists know that with an indifferent degree they'll get a comfortable job, while their contemporaries and counterparts in English or History will be lucky to earn 60 per cent as much. No young scientist of any talent would feel that he isn't wanted or that his work is ridiculous, as did the hero of *Lucky Jim*, and in fact, some of the disgruntlement of Amis and his associates is the disgruntlement of the under-employed arts graduate.

There is only one way out of all this: it is, of course, by rethinking our education. In this country, for the two reasons I have given, that is more difficult than in any other. Nearly everyone will agree that our school education is too specialised. But nearly everyone feels that it is outside the will of man to alter it. Other countries are as dissatisfied with their education as we are, but are not so resigned.

The U.S. teach out of proportion more children up to eighteen than we do: they teach them far more widely, but nothing like so rigorously. They know that: they are hoping to take the problem in hand within ten years, though they may not have all that time to spare. The U.S.S.R. also teach out of proportion more children than we do: they also teach far more widely than we do (it is an absurd western myth that their school education is specialised) but much too rigorously.[11] They know that—and they are beating about to get it right. The Scandinavians, in particular the Swedes, who would make a more sensible job of it than any of us, are handicapped by their practical need to devote an inordinate amount of time to foreign languages. But they too are seized of the problem.

Are we? Have we crystallised so far that we are no longer flexible at all?

Talk to schoolmasters, and they say that our intense specialisation, like nothing else on earth, is dictated by the Oxford and Cambridge scholarship examinations. If that is so, one would have thought it not utterly impracticable to change the Oxford and Cambridge scholarship examinations. Yet one would underestimate the national capacity for the intricate defensive to believe that that was easy. All the lessons of our educational history suggest we are only capable of increasing specialisation, not decreasing it.

Somehow we have set ourselves the task of producing a tiny *élite*—far smaller proportionately than in any comparable country—educated in one academic skill. For a hundred and fifty years in Cambridge it was mathematics: then it was mathematics or classics: then natural science was allowed in. But still the choice had to be a single one.

It may well be that this process has gone too far to be reversible. I have given reasons why I think it is a disastrous process, for the purpose of a living culture. I am going on to give reasons why I think it is fatal, if we're to perform our practical tasks in the world. But I can think of only one example, in the whole of English educational history, where our pursuit of specialised mental exercises was resisted with success.

It was done here in Cambridge, fifty years ago, when the old order-of-merit in the Mathematical Tripos was abolished. For over a hundred years, the nature of the Tripos had been crystallising. The competition for the top places had got fiercer, and careers hung on them. In most colleges, certainly in my own, if one managed to come out as Senior or Second Wrangler, one was elected a Fellow out of hand. A whole apparatus of coaching had grown up. Men of the quality of Hardy, Littlewood, Russell, Eddington, Jeans, Keynes, went in for two or three years' training for an examination which was intensely competitive and intensely difficult. Most people in Cambridge were very proud of it, with a similar pride to that which almost anyone in England always has for our existing educational institutions, whatever they happen to be. If you study the fly-sheets of the time, you will find the passionate arguments for keeping the examination precisely as it was to all eternity: it was the only way to keep up standards, it was the only fair test of merit, indeed, the only seriously objective test in the world. The arguments, in fact, were almost exactly those which are used today with precisely the same passionate sincerity if anyone suggests that the scholarship examinations might conceivably not be immune from change.

In every respect but one, in fact, the old Mathematical Tripos seemed perfect. The one exception, however, appeared to some to be rather important. It was simply—so the young creative mathematicians, such as Hardy and Littlewood, kept saying—that the training had no intellectual merit at all. They went a little further, and said that the Tripos had killed serious mathematics in England stone dead for a hundred years. Well, even in academic controversy, that took some skirting round, and they got their way. But I have an impression that Cambridge was a good deal more flexible between 1850 and 1914 than it has been in our time. If we had had the old Mathematical Tripos firmly planted among us, should we have ever managed to abolish it?

2

INTELLECTUALS AS NATURAL LUDDITES

The reasons for the existence of the two cultures are many, deep, and complex, some rooted in social histories, some in personal histories, and some in the inner dynamic of the different kinds of mental activity themselves. But I want to isolate one which is not so much a reason as a correlative, something which winds in and out of any of these discussions. It can be said simply, and it is this. If we forget the scientific culture, then the rest of western intellectuals have never tried, wanted, or been able to understand the industrial revolution, much less accept it. Intellectuals, in particular literary intellectuals, are natural Luddites.

That is specially true of this country, where the industrial revolution happened to us earlier than elsewhere, during a long spell of absentmindedness. Perhaps that helps explain our present degree of crystallisation. But, with a little qualification, it is also true, and surprisingly true, of the United States.

In both countries, and indeed all over the West, the first wave of the industrial revolution crept on, without anyone noticing what was happening. It was, of course—or at least it was destined to become, under our own eyes, and in our own time—by far the biggest transformation in society since the discovery of agriculture. In fact, those two revolutions, the agricultural and the industrial-scientific, are the only qualitative changes in social living that men have ever known. But the traditional culture didn't notice: or when it did notice, didn't like what it saw. Not that the traditional culture wasn't doing extremely well out of the revolution; the English educational institutions took their slice of the English nineteenth-century wealth, and perversely, it helped crystallise them in the forms we know.

Almost none of the talent, almost none of the imaginative energy, went back into the revolution which was producing the wealth. The traditional culture became more abstracted from it as it became more wealthy, trained its young men for administration, for the Indian Empire, for the purpose of perpetuating the culture itself, but never in any circumstances to equip them to understand the revolution or take part in it. Far-sighted men were beginning to see, before the middle of the nineteenth century, that in order to go on producing wealth, the country needed to train some of its bright minds in science, particularly in applied science. No one listened. The traditional culture didn't listen at all: and the pure scientists, such as there were, didn't listen very eagerly. You will find the story, which in spirit continues down to the present day, in Eric Ashby's *Technology and the Academics.*[12]

The academics had nothing to do with the industrial revolution; as Corrie, the old Master of Jesus, said about trains running into Cambridge on Sunday, 'It is equally displeasing to God and to myself'. So far as there was any thinking in nineteenth-century industry, it was left to cranks and clever workmen. American social historians have told me that much the same was true of the U.S. The industrial revolution, which began developing in New England fifty years or so later than ours,[13] apparently received very little educated talent, either then or later in the nineteenth century. It had to make do with the guidance handymen could give it—sometimes, of course, handymen like Henry Ford, with a dash of genius.

The curious thing was that in Germany, in the 1830's and 1840's, long before .serious industrialisation had started there, it was possible to get a good university education in applied science, better than anything England or the U.S. could offer for a couple of generations. I don't begin to understand this: it doesn't make social sense: but it was so. With the result that Ludwig Mond, the son of a court purveyor, went to Heidelberg and learnt some sound applied chemistry. Siemens, a Prussian signals officer, at military academy and university went through what for their time were excellent courses in electrical engineering. Then they came to England, met no competition at all, brought in other educated Germans, and made fortunes exactly as though they were dealing with a rich, illiterate colonial territory. Similar fortunes were made by German technologists in the United States.

Almost everywhere, though, intellectual persons didn't comprehend what was happening. Certainly the writers didn't. Plenty of them shuddered away, as though the right course for a man of feeling was to contract out; some, like Ruskin and William Morris and Thoreau and Emerson and Lawrence, tried various kinds of fancies which were not in effect more than screams of horror. It is hard to think of a writer of high class who really stretched his imaginative sympathy, who could see at once the hideous back-streets, the smoking chimneys, the internal price—and also the prospects of life that were opening out for the poor, the intimations, up to now unknown except to the lucky, which were just coming within reach of the remaining 99.0 per cent of his brother men. Some of the nineteenth-century Russian novelists might have done; their natures were broad enough; but they were living in a pre-industrial society and didn't have the opportunity. The only writer of world class who seems to have had an understanding of the industrial revolution was Ibsen in his old age: and there wasn't much that old man didn't understand.

For, of course, one truth is straightforward. Industrialisation is the only hope of the poor. I use the word 'hope' in a crude and prosaic sense. I have not much use for the moral sensibility of anyone who is too refined to use it so. It is all very well for us, sitting pretty, to think that material standards of living don't matter all that much. It is all very well for one, as a personal choice, to reject industrialisation—do a modern Walden, if you like, and if you go without much food, see most of your children die in infancy, despise the comforts of literacy, accept twenty years off your own life, then I respect you for the strength of your aesthetic revulsion.[14] But I don't respect you in the slightest if, even passively, you try to impose the same choice on others who are not free to choose. In fact, we know what their choice would be. For, with singular unanimity, in any country where they have had the chance, the poor have walked off the land into the factories as fast as the factories could take them.

I remember talking to my grandfather when I was a child. He was a good specimen of a nineteenth-century artisan. He was highly intelligent, and he had a great deal of character. He had left school at the age of ten, and had educated himself intensely until he was an old man. He had all his class's passionate faith in education. Yet, he had never had the luck—or, as I now suspect, the worldly force and dexterity—to go very far. In fact, he never went further than maintenance foreman in a tramway depot. His life would seem to his grandchildren laborious and unrewarding almost beyond belief. But it didn't seem to him quite like that. He was much too sensible a man not to know that he hadn't been adequately used: he had too much pride not to feel a proper rancour: he was disappointed that he had not done more—and yet, compared with *his* grandfather, he felt he had done a lot. His grandfather must have been an agricultural labourer. I don't so much as know his Christian name. He was one of the 'dark people', as the old Russian liberals used to call them, completely lost in the great anonymous sludge of history. So far as my grandfather knew, he could not read or write. He was a man of ability, my grandfather thought; my grandfather was pretty unforgiving about what society had done, or not done, to his ancestors, and did not romanticise their state. It was no fun being an agricultural labourer in the mid to late eighteenth century, in the time that we, snobs that we are, think of only as the time of the Enlightenment and Jane Austen.

The industrial revolution looked very different according to whether one saw it from above or below. It looks very different today according to whether one sees it from Chelsea or from a village in Asia. To people like my grandfather, there was no question that the industrial revolution was less bad than what had gone before. The only question was, how to make it better.

In a more sophisticated sense, that is still the question. In the advanced countries, we have realised in a rough and ready way what the old industrial revolution brought with it. A great increase of population, because applied science went hand in hand with medical science and medical care. Enough to eat, for a similar reason. Everyone able to read and write, because an industrial society can't work without. Health, food, education; nothing but the industrial revolution could have spread them right down to the very poor. Those are primary gains—there are losses[15] too, of course, one of which is that organising a society for industry makes it easy to organise it for all-out war. But the gains remain. They are the base of our social hope.

And yet: do we understand how they have happened? Have we begun to comprehend even the old industrial revolution? Much less the new scientific revolution in which we stand? There never was anything more necessary to comprehend.

3

THE SCIENTIFIC REVOLUTION

I have just mentioned a distinction between the industrial revolution and the scientific revolution. The distinction is not clear-edged, but it is a useful one, and I ought to try to define it now. By the industrial revolution, I mean the gradual use of machines, the employment of men and women in factories, the change in this country from a population mainly of agricultural labourers to a population mainly engaged in making things in factories and distributing them when they were made. That change, as I have said, crept on us unawares, untouched by academics, hated by Luddites, practical Luddites and intellectual ones. It is connected, so it seems to me, with many of the attitudes to science and aesthetics which have crystallised among us. One can date it roughly from the middle of the eighteenth century to the early twentieth. Out of it grew another change, closely related to the first, but far more deeply scientific, far quicker, and probably far more prodigious in its result. This change comes from the application of real science to industry, no longer hit and miss, no longer the ideas of odd 'inventors', but the real stuff.

Dating this second change is very largely a matter of taste. Some would prefer to go back to the first large-scale chemical or engineering industries, round about sixty years ago. For myself, I should put it much further on, not earlier than thirty to forty years ago— and as a rough definition, I should take the time when atomic particles were first made industrial use of. I believe the industrial society of electronics, atomic energy, automation, is in cardinal respects different in kind from any that has gone before, and will change the world much more. It is this transformation that, in my view, is entitled to the name of 'scientific revolution'.

This is the material basis for our lives: or more exactly, the social plasma of which we are a part. And we know almost nothing about it. I remarked earlier that the highly educated members of the non-scientific culture couldn't cope with the simplest concepts of pure science: it is unexpected, but they would be even less happy with applied science. How many educated people know anything about productive industry, old-style or new? What is a machine-tool? I once asked a literary party; and they looked shifty. Unless one knows, industrial production is as mysterious as witch-doctoring. Or take buttons. Buttons aren't very complicated things: they are being made in millions every day: one has to be a reasonably ferocious Luddite not to think that that is, on the whole, an estimable activity. Yet I would bet that out of men getting firsts in arts subjects at Cambridge this year, not one in ten could give the loosest analysis of the human organisation which it needs.

In the United States, perhaps, there is a wider nodding acquaintance with industry, but, now I come to think of it, no American novelist of any class has ever been able to assume that his audience had it. He can assume, and only too often does, an acquaintance with a pseudo-feudal society, like the fag-end of the Old South—but not with industrial society. Certainly an English novelist couldn't.

Yet the personal relations in a productive organisation are of the greatest subtlety and interest. They are very deceptive. They look as though they ought to be the personal relations that one gets in any hierarchical structure with a chain of command, like a division in the army or a department in the Civil Service. In practice they are much more complex than that, and anyone used to the straight chain of command gets lost the instant he sets foot in an industrial organisation. No one in any country, incidentally, knows yet what these personal relations ought to be. That is a problem almost independent of large-scale politics, a problem springing straight out of the industrial life.

I think it is only fair to say that most pure scientists have themselves been devastatingly ignorant of productive industry, and many still are. It is permissible to lump pure and applied scientists into the same scientific culture, but the gaps are wide. Pure scientists and engineers often totally misunderstand each other. Their behaviour tends to be very different: engineers have to live their lives in an organised community, and however odd they are underneath they manage to present a disciplined face to the world. Not so pure scientists. In the same way pure scientists still, though less than twenty years ago, have statistically a higher proportion in politics left of centre than any other profession: not so engineers, who are conservative almost to a man. Not reactionary in the extreme literary sense, but just conservative. They are absorbed in making things, and the present social order is good enough for them.

Pure scientists have by and large been dim-witted about engineers and applied science. They couldn't get interested. They wouldn't recognise that many of the problems were as intellectually exacting as pure problems, and that many of the solutions were as satisfying and beautiful. Their instinct—perhaps sharpened in this country by the passion to find a new snobbism wherever possible, and to invent one if it doesn't exist —was to take it for granted that applied science was an occupation for second-rate minds. I say this more sharply because thirty years ago I took precisely that line myself. The climate of thought of young research workers in Cambridge then was not to our credit. We prided ourselves that the science we were doing could not, in any conceivable circumstances, have any practical use. The more firmly one could make that claim, the more superior one felt.

Rutherford himself had little feeling for engineering. He was amazed—he used to relate the story with incredulous admiration—that Kapitza had actually sent an engineering drawing to Metrovick, and that those magicians had duly studied the drawing, *made the machine*, and delivered it in Kapitza's laboratory! Rutherford was so impressed by Cockcroft's engineering skill that he secured for him a special capital grant for machinery—the grant was as much as six hundred pounds! In 1933, four years before his death, Rutherford said, firmly and explicitly, that he didn't believe the energy of the nucleus would ever be released—nine years later, at Chicago, the first pile began to run. That was the only major bloomer in scientific judgment Rutherford ever made. It is interesting that it should be at the point where pure science turned into applied.

No, pure scientists did not show much understanding or display much sense of social fact. The best that can be said for them is that, given the necessity, they found it fairly easy to learn. In the war, a great many scientists had to learn, for the good Johnsonian reason that sharpens one's wits, something about productive industry. It opened their eyes. In my own job, I had to try to get some insight into industry. It was one of the most valuable pieces of education in my life. But it started when I was thirty-five, and I ought to have had it much earlier.

That brings me back to education. Why aren't we coping with the scientific revolution? Why are other countries doing better? How are we going to meet our future, both our cultural and practical future? It should be obvious by now that I believe both lines of argument lead to the same end. If one begins by thinking only of the intellectual life, or only of the

33

social life, one comes to a point where it becomes manifest that our education has gone wrong, and gone wrong in the same way.

I don't pretend that any country has got its education perfect. In some ways, as I said before, the Russians and Americans are both more actively dissatisfied with theirs than we are: that is, they are taking more drastic steps to change it. But that is because they are more sensitive to the world they are living in. For myself, I have no doubt that, though neither of them have got the answer right, they are a good deal nearer than we are. We do some things much better than either of them. In educational tactics, we are often more gifted than they are. In educational strategy, by their side we are only playing at it.

The differences between the three systems are revelatory. We teach, of course, a far smaller proportion of our children up to the age of eighteen: and we take a far smaller proportion even of those we do teach up to the level of a university degree. The old pattern of training a small *élite* has never been broken, though it has been slightly bent. Within that pattern, we have kept the national passion for specialisation: and we work our clever young up to the age of twenty-one far harder than the Americans, though no harder than the Russians. At eighteen, our science specialists know more science than their contemporaries anywhere, though they know less of anything else. At twenty-one, when they take their first degree they are probably still a year or so ahead.

34

The American strategy is different in kind. They take everyone, the entire population,[16] up to eighteen in high schools, and educate them very loosely and generally. Their problem is to inject some rigour—in particular some fundamental mathematics and science —into this loose education. A very large proportion of the eighteen-year-olds then go to college: and this college education is, like the school education, much more diffuse and less professional than ours.[17] At the end of four years, the young men and women are usually not so well-trained professionally as we are: though I think it is fair comment to say that a higher proportion of the best of them, having been run on a looser rein, retain their creative zest. Real severity enters with the Ph.D. At that level the Americans suddenly begin to work their students much harder than we do. It is worth remembering that they find enough talent to turn out nearly as many Ph.D.s in science and engineering each year as we contrive to get through our first degrees.

The Russian high school education is much less specialised than ours, much more arduous than the American. It is so arduous that for the non-academic it seems to have proved too tough, and they are trying other methods from fifteen to seventeen. The general method has been to put everyone through a kind of continental Lycée course, with a sizeable component, more than 40 per cent, of science and mathematics. Everyone has to do all subjects. At the university this general education ceases abruptly: and for the last three years of the five-year course the specialisation is more intensive even than ours. That is, at most English universities a young man can take an honours degree in mechanical engineering. In Russia he can take, and an enormous number do take, a corresponding degree in one bit of mechanical engineering, as it might be aerodynamics or machine-tool design or diesel engine production.

They won't listen to me, but I believe they have overdone this, just as I believe they have slightly overdone the number of engineers they are training. It is now much larger than the rest of the world put together—getting on for fifty per cent larger.[18] Pure scientists they are training only slightly more than the United States, though in physics and mathematics the balance is heavily in the Russian direction.

Our population is small by the side of either the U.S.A. or the U.S.S.R. Roughly, if we compare like with like, and put scientists and engineers together, we are training at a professional level per head of the population one Englishman to every one and a half Americans to every two and a half Russians.[19] Someone is wrong.

With some qualifications, I believe the Russians have judged the situation sensibly. They have a deeper insight into the scientific revolution than we have, or than the Americans have. The gap between the cultures doesn't seem to be anything like so wide as with us. If one reads contemporary Soviet novels, for example, one finds that their novelists can assume in their audience—as we cannot—at least a rudimentary acquaintance with what industry is all about. Pure science doesn't often come in, and they don't appear much happier with it than literary intellectuals are here. But engineering does come in. An engineer in a Soviet novel is as acceptable, so it seems, as a psychiatrist in an American one. They are as ready to cope in art with the processes of production as Balzac was with the processes of craft manufacture. I don't want to overstress this, but it may be significant. It may also be significant that, in these novels, one is constantly coming up against a passionate belief in education. The people in them believe in education exactly as my grandfather did, and for the same mixture of idealistic and bread-and-butter reasons.

Anyway, the Russians have judged what kind and number of educated men and women[20] a country needs to come out top in the scientific revolution. I am going to oversimplify, but their estimate, and I believe it's pretty near right, is this. First of all, as many alpha plus scientists as the country can throw up. No country has many of them. Provided the schools and universities are there, it doesn't matter all that much what you teach them. They will look after themselves.[21] We probably have at least as many pro-rata as the Russians and Americans; that is the least of our worries. Second, a much larger stratum of alpha professionals—these are the people who are going to do the supporting research, the high class design and development. In quality, England compares well in this stratum with the U.S.A. or U.S.S.R.: this is what our education is specially geared to produce. In quantity, though, we are not discovering (again per head of the population) half as many as the Russians think necessary and are able to find. Third, another stratum, educated to about the level of Part I of the Natural Sciences or Mechanical Sciences Tripos, or perhaps slightly below that. Some of these will do the secondary technical jobs, but some will take major responsibility, particularly in the human jobs. The proper use of such men depends upon a different distribution of ability from the one that has grown up here. As the scientific revolution goes on, the call for these men will be something we haven't imagined, though the Russians have. They will be required in thousands upon thousands, and they will need all the human development that university education can give them.[22] It is here, perhaps, most of all that our insight has been fogged. Fourthly and last, politicians, administrators, an entire community, who know enough science to have a sense of what the scientists are talking about.

That, or something like that, is the specification for the scientific revolution.[23] I wish I were certain that in this country we were adaptable enough to meet it. In a moment I want to go on to an issue which will, in the world view, count more: but perhaps I can be forgiven for taking a sideways look at our own fate. It happens that of all the advanced countries, our position is by a long way the most precarious. That is the result of history and accident, and isn't to be laid to the blame of any Englishman now living. If our ancestors had invested talent in the industrial revolution instead of the Indian Empire, we might be more soundly based now. But they didn't.

We are left with a population twice as large as we can grow food for, so that we are always going to be *au fond* more anxious than France or Sweden:[24] and with very little in the way of natural resources—by the standard of the great world powers, with nothing. The only real assets we have, in fact, are our wits. Those have served us pretty well, in two ways. We have a good deal of cunning, native or acquired, in the arts of getting on among ourselves: that is a strength. And we have been inventive and creative, possibly out of proportion to our numbers. I don't believe much in national differences in cleverness, but compared with other countries we are certainly no stupider.

Given these two assets, and they are our only ones, it should have been for us to understand the scientific revolution first, to educate ourselves to the limit and give a lead. Well, we have done something. In some fields, like atomic energy, we have done better than anyone could have predicted. Within the pattern, the rigid and crystallised pattern of our education and of the two cultures, we have been trying moderately hard to adjust ourselves.

The bitterness is, it is nothing like enough. To say we have to educate ourselves or perish, is a little more melodramatic than the facts warrant. To say, we have to educate ourselves or watch a steep decline in our own lifetime, is about right. We can't do it, I am now convinced, without breaking the existing pattern. I know how difficult this is. It goes against the emotional grain of nearly all of us. In many ways, it goes against my own, standing uneasily with one foot in a dead or dying world and the other in a world that at all costs we must see born. I wish I could be certain that we shall have the courage of what our minds tell us.

More often than I like, I am saddened by a historical myth. Whether the myth is good history or not, doesn't matter; it is pressing enough for me. I can't help thinking of the Venetian Republic in their last half-century. Like us, they had once been fabulously lucky. They had become rich, as we did, by accident. They had acquired immense political skill, just as we have. A good many of them were tough-minded, realistic, patriotic men. They knew, just as clearly as we know, that the current of history had begun to flow against them. Many of them gave their minds to working out ways to keep going. It would have meant breaking the pattern into which they had crystallised. They were fond of the pattern, just as we are fond of ours. They never found the will to break it.

4

THE RICH AND THE POOR

But that is our local problem, and it is for us to struggle
with it. Sometimes, it is true, I have felt that the
Venetian shadow falls over the entire West. I have
felt that on the other side of the Mississippi. In more
resilient moments, I comfort myself that Americans
are much more like us between 1850 and 1914. Whatever they don't do, they do react. It's going to take
them a long and violent pull to be as well prepared for
the scientific revolution as the Russians are, but there
are good chances that they will do it.

Nevertheless, that isn't the main issue of the scientific
revolution. The main issue is that the people in the
industrialised countries are getting richer, and those in
the non-industrialised countries are at best standing
still: so that the gap between the industrialised countries
and the rest is widening every day. On the world scale
this is the gap between the rich and the poor.

Among the rich are the U.S., the white Common-
wealth countries, Great Britain, most of Europe, and
the U.S.S.R. China is betwixt and between, not yet
over the industrial hump, but probably getting there.
The poor are all the rest. In the rich countries people
are living longer, eating better, working less. In a poor
country like India, the expectation of life is less than

half what it is in England. There is some evidence that Indians and other Asians are eating less, in absolute quantities, than they were a generation ago. The statistics are not reliable, and informants in the F.A.O. have told me not to put much trust in them. But it is accepted that, in all non-industrialised countries, people are not eating better than at the subsistence level. And they are working as people have always had to work, from Neolithic times until our own. Life for the overwhelming majority of mankind has always been nasty, brutish and short. It is so in the poor countries still.

This disparity between the rich and the poor has been noticed. It has been noticed, most acutely and not unnaturally, by the poor. Just because they have noticed it, it won't last for long. Whatever else in the world we know survives to the year 2000, that won't. Once the trick of getting rich is known, as it now is, the world can't survive half rich and half poor. It's just not on.

The West has got to help in this transformation. The trouble is, the West with its divided culture finds it hard to grasp just how big, and above all just how fast, the transformation must be.

Earlier I said that few non-scientists really understand the scientific concept of acceleration. I meant that as a gibe. But in social terms, it is a little more than a gibe. During all human history until this century, the rate of social change has been very slow. So slow, that it would pass unnoticed in one person's lifetime. That is no longer so. The rate of change has increased so much that our imagination can't keep up. There is *bound* to be more social change, affecting more people, in the next decade than in any before. There is *bound* to be more change again, in the 1970's. In the poor countries, people have caught on to this simple concept. Men there are no longer prepared to wait for periods longer than one person's lifetime.

The comforting assurances, given *de haut en bas*, that maybe in a hundred or two hundred years things may be slightly better for them—they only madden. Pronouncements such as one still hears from old Asia or old Africa hands—Why, it will take those people five hundred years to get up to our standard!—they are both suicidal and technologically illiterate. Particularly when said, as they always seem to be said, by someone looking as though it wouldn't take Neanderthal Man five years to catch up with *him*.

The fact is, the rate of change has already been proved possible. Someone said, when the first atomic bomb went off, that the only important secret is now let out—the thing works. After that, any determined country could make the bomb, given a few years. In the same way, the only secret of the Russian and Chinese industrialisation is that they've brought it off. That is what Asians and Africans have noticed. It took the Russians about forty years, starting with something of an industrial base—Tsarist industry wasn't negligible—but interrupted by a civil war and then the greatest war of all. The Chinese started with much less of an industrial base, but haven't been interrupted, and

43

it looks like taking them not much over half the time.

These transformations were made with inordinate effort and with great suffering. Much of the suffering was unnecessary: the horror is hard to look at straight, standing in the same decades. Yet they've proved that common men can show astonishing fortitude in chasing jam tomorrow. Jam today, and men aren't at their most exciting: jam tomorrow, and one often sees them at their noblest. The transformations have also proved something which only the scientific culture can take in its stride. Yet, when we don't take it in our stride, it makes us look silly.

It is simply that technology is rather easy. Or more exactly, technology is the branch of human experience that people can learn with predictable results. For a long time, the West misjudged this very badly. After all, a good many Englishmen have been skilled in mechanical crafts for half-a-dozen generations. Somehow we've made ourselves believe that the whole of technology was a more or less incommunicable art. It's true enough, we start with a certain advantage. Not so much because of tradition, I think, as because all our children play with mechanical toys. They are picking up pieces of applied science before they can read. That is an advantage we haven't made the most of. Just as the Americans have the advantage that nine out of ten adults can drive a car and are to some extent mechanics. In the last war, which was a war of small machines, that was a real military asset. Russia is catching up with the U.S. in major industry—but it will be a long time before Russia is as convenient a country as the U.S. in which to have one's car break down.[25]

The curious thing is, none of that seems to matter much. For the task of totally industrialising a major country, as in China today, it only takes will to train enough scientists and engineers and technicians. Will, and quite a small number of years. There is no evidence that any country or race is better than any other in scientific teachability: there is a good deal of evidence that all are much alike. Tradition and technical background seem to count for surprisingly little.

We've all seen this with our own eyes. I myself have found Sicilian girls taking the top places in the Honours Physics course—a very exacting course—at the University of Rome: they'd have been in something like purdah thirty years ago. And I remember John Cockcroft coming back from Moscow some time in the early 1930's. The news got round that he had been able to have a look, not only at laboratories, but at factories and the mechanics in them. What we expected to hear, I don't know: but there were certainly some who had pleasurable expectations of those stories precious to the hearts of western man, about moujiks prostrating themselves before a milling machine, or breaking a vertical borer with their bare hands. Someone asked Cockcroft what the skilled workmen were like. Well, he has never been a man to waste words. A fact is a fact is a fact. 'Oh,' he said, 'they're just about the same as the ones at Metrovick.' That was all. He was, as usual, right.

There is no getting away from it. It is technically possible to carry out the scientific revolution in India, Africa, South-east Asia, Latin America, the Middle East, within fifty years. There is no excuse for western man not to know this. And not to know that this is the one way out through the three menaces which stand in our way—H-bomb war, over-population, the gap between the rich and the poor. This is one of the situations where the worst crime is innocence.

Since the gap between the rich countries and the poor can be removed, it will be. If we are short-sighted, inept, incapable either of good-will or en-lightened self-interest, then it may be removed to the accompaniment of war and starvation: but removed it will be. The questions are, how, and by whom. To those questions, one can only give partial answers: but that may be enough to set us thinking. The scientific revolution on the world-scale needs, first and fore-most, capital: capital in all forms, including capital machinery. The poor countries, until they have got beyond a certain point on the industrial curve cannot accumulate that capital. That is why the gap between rich and poor is widening. The capital must come from outside.

There are only two possible sources. One is the West, which means mainly the U.S., the other is the U.S.S.R. Even the United States hasn't infinite re-sources of such capital. If they or Russia tried to do it alone, it would mean an effort greater than either had to make industrially in the war. If they both took part, it wouldn't mean that order of sacrifice—though in my view it's optimistic to think, as some wise men do, that it would mean no sacrifice at all. The scale of the operation requires that it would have to be a national one. Private industry, even the biggest private industry, can't touch it, and in no sense is it a fair business risk. It's a bit like asking Duponts or I.C.I. back in 1940 to finance the entire development of the atomic bomb.

The second requirement, after capital, as important as capital, is men. That is, trained scientists and engineers adaptable enough to devote themselves to a foreign country's industrialisation for at least ten years out of their lives. Here, unless and until the Americans and we educate ourselves both sensibly and imaginatively, the Russians have a clear edge. This is where their educational policy has already paid big dividends. They have such men to spare if they are needed. We just haven't, and the Americans aren't much better off. Imagine, for example, that the U.S. government and ours had agreed to help the Indians to carry out a major industrialisation, similar in scale to the Chinese. Imagine that the capital could be found. It would then require something like ten thousand to twenty thousand engineers from the U.S. and here to help get the thing going. At present, we couldn't find them.

These men, whom we don't yet possess, need to be trained not only in scientific but in human terms. They could not do their job if they did not shrug off every trace of paternalism. Plenty of Europeans, from St Francis Xavier to Schweitzer, have devoted their lives to Asians and Africans, nobly but paternally. These are not the Europeans whom Asians and Africans are going to welcome now. They want men who will muck in as colleagues, who will pass on what they know, do an honest technical job, and get out. Fortunately, this is an attitude which comes easily to scientists. They are freer than most people from racial feeling; their own culture is in its human relations a democratic one. In their own internal climate, the breeze of the equality of man hits you in the face, sometimes rather roughly, just as it does in Norway.

That is why scientists would do us good all over Asia and Africa. And they would do their part too in the third essential of the scientific revolution—which, in a country like India, would have to run in parallel with the capital investment and the initial foreign help. That is, an educational programme as complete as the Chinese, who appear in ten years to have transformed their universities and built so many new ones that they are now nearly independent of scientists and engineers from outside. Ten years. With scientific teachers from this country and the U.S., and what is also necessary, with teachers of English, other poor countries could do the same in twenty.

That is the size of the problem. An immense capital outlay, an immense investment in men, both scientists and linguists, most of whom the West does not yet possess. With rewards negligible in the short term, apart from doing the job: and in the long term most uncertain.

People will ask me, in fact in private they have already asked me—'This is all very fine and large. But you are supposed to be a realistic man. You are interested in the fine structure of politics; you have spent some time studying how men behave in the pursuit of their own ends. Can you possibly believe that men will behave as you say they ought to? Can you imagine a political technique, in parliamentary societies like the U.S. or our own, by which any such plan could become real? Do you really believe that there is one chance in ten that any of this will happen?'

That is fair comment. I can only reply that I don't know. On the one hand, it is a mistake, and it is a mistake, of course, which anyone who is called realistic is specially liable to fall into, to think that when we have said something about the egotisms, the weaknesses, the vanities, the power-seekings of men, that we have said everything. Yes, they are like that. They are the bricks with which we have got to build, and one can judge them through the extent of one's own selfishness. But they are sometimes capable of more, and any 'realism' which doesn't admit of that isn't serious.

On the other hand, I confess, and I should be less than honest if I didn't, that I can't see the political techniques through which the good human capabilities of the West can get into action. The best one can do, and it is a poor best, is to nag away. That is perhaps too easy a palliative for one's disquiet: For, though I don't know how we can do what we need to do, or whether we shall do anything at all, I do know this: that, if we don't do it, the Communist countries will in time. They will do it at great cost to themselves and others, but they will do it. If that is how it turns out, we shall have failed, both practically and morally. At best, the West will have become an *enclave* in a different world—and this country will be the *enclave* of an *enclave*. Are we resigning ourselves to that? History is merciless to failure. In any case, if that happens, we shall not be writing the history.

Meanwhile, there are steps to be taken which aren't outside the powers of reflective people. Education isn't the total solution to this problem: but without education the West can't even begin to cope. All the arrows point the same way. Closing the gap between our cultures is a necessity in the most abstract intellectual sense, as well as in the most practical. When those two senses have grown apart, then no society is going to be able to think with wisdom. For the sake of the intellectual life, for the sake of this country's special danger, for the sake of the western society living precariously rich among the poor, for the sake of the poor who needn't be poor if there is intelligence in the world, it is obligatory for us and the Americans and the whole West to look at our education with fresh eyes. This is one of the cases where we and the Americans have the most to learn from each other. We have each a good deal to learn from the Russians, if we are not too proud. Incidentally, the Russians have a good deal to learn from us, too.

Isn't it time we began? The danger is, we have been brought up to think as though we had all the time in the world. We have very little time. So little that I dare not guess at it.

II. THE TWO CULTURES:
A SECOND LOOK

§ 1

IT is over four years since (in May 1959) I gave the Rede Lecture at Cambridge. I chose a subject which several of us had been discussing for some time past. I hoped at most to act as a goad to action, first in education and second—in my own mind the latter part of the lecture was always the more pressing —in sharpening the concern of rich and privileged societies for those less lucky. I did not expect much. Plenty of people were saying similar things. It seemed to me to be a time when one should add one's voice. I thought I might be listened to in some restricted circles. Then the effect would soon die down: and in due course, since I was deeply committed, I should feel obliged to have another go.

For a while that appeared to be a reasonable prognosis. According to precedent, the lecture was published, as a paper-covered pamphlet,[26] the day after it was delivered. It received some editorial attention, but, in the first months, not many reviews. There was not, and could not be, any advertising. *Encounter* published long extracts, and these drew some comment.[27] I had a number of interesting private letters. That, I thought, was the end of it.

It did not turn out quite like that. By the end of the first year I began to feel uncomfortably like the sorcerer's apprentice. Articles, references, letters, blame, praise, were floating in—often from countries where I was otherwise unknown. The whole phenomenon, in fact, as I shall shortly explain, hadn't much connection with me. It was a curious, rather than a pleasurable, experience. The literature has gone on accumulating at an accelerating pace: I suppose I must, by the nature of things, have seen more of it than anyone else; but I have not seen anything like the whole. And it is frustrating to be told that some of the more valuable discussions have been taking place in languages not accessible to most Englishmen, such as Hungarian, Polish and Japanese.

As the flood of literature mounted, two deductions became self-evident. The first was that if a nerve had been touched almost simultaneously in different intellectual societies, in different parts of the world, the ideas which produced this response couldn't possibly be original. Original ideas don't carry at that speed. Very occasionally one thinks or hopes that one has said something new: and waits a little bleakly for years, in the hope that it will strike a spark of recognition somewhere. This was quite different. It was clear that many people had been thinking on this assembly of topics. The ideas were in the air. Anyone, anywhere, had only to choose a form of words. Then—click, the trigger was pressed. The words need not be the right words: but the time, which no-one could predict beforehand, had to be the right time. When that happened, the sorcerer's apprentice was left to look at the water rushing in.

It seems to be pure chance that others had not found themselves, some time earlier, in the same apprentice-like position. Jacob Bronowski had, at various times in the fifties,[28] dealt imaginatively with many aspects of these problems. Merle Kling in 1957 published an article[29]—unknown to me until much later—which closely anticipated the first half of my lecture. Professional educators such as A. D. C. Peterson had done much the same. In 1956[30] and 1957[31] I myself wrote two pieces which, though shorter than the Rede Lecture, contained much of its substance. Yet none of us got much response. Two years later the time was right; and any one of us could have produced a hubbub. It is a reminder of the mysterious operation of what, in the nineteenth century, was reverently referred to as the *Zeitgeist*.

The first deduction, then, is that these ideas were not at all original, but were waiting in the air. The second deduction is, I think, equally obvious. It is, that there must be something in them. I don't mean that they are necessarily right; I don't mean that they couldn't have been expressed in many different or better forms: but contained in them or hidden beneath them, there is something which people, all over the world, suspect is relevant to present actions. It would not have mattered whether these things were said by me or Bronowski or Kling, or A or B or C. A complex argument started, and will go on. This could not have happened adventitiously. It certainly could not have happened through any personal impact. On these issues our personalities mean nothing: but the issues themselves mean a good deal.

The sheer volume of comment has been formidable, some of it agreeing with me, some cross-bench, and some disagreeing. Many of the criticisms I respect. I have not replied to them piecemeal, since I have been following a rule which I have set myself in other controversies. It seems to me that engaging in immediate debate on each specific point closes one's own mind for good and all. Debating gives most of us much more psychological satisfaction than thinking does: but it deprives us of whatever chance there is of getting closer to the truth. It seems preferable to me to sit back and let what has been said sink in—I don't pretend this is altogether easy—and then, after a longish interval, with the advantage of what I have heard and of new knowledge, see what modifications I should make if I were going to give the lecture again. This is what I am doing now. I intend to continue the same practice in the future. If I think I have anything further to add, I shall leave it for some time.

During the arguments so far, there has been one unusual manifestation, which I shall mention just to get it out of the way. A few, a very few, of the criticisms have been loaded with personal abuse to an abnormal extent: to such an extent in one case, in fact, that the persons responsible for its publication in two different media[32] made separate approaches to me, in order to obtain my consent. I had to assure them that I did not propose to take legal action. All this seemed to me distinctly odd. In any dispute acrimonious words are likely to fly about, but it is not common, at least in my experience, for them to come anywhere near the limit of defamation.

However, the problem of behaviour in these circumstances is very easily solved. Let us imagine that I am called, in print, a kleptomaniac necrophilist (I have selected with some care two allegations which have not, so far as I know, been made). I have exactly two courses of action. The first, and the one which in general I should choose to follow, is to do precisely nothing. The second is, if the nuisance becomes intolerable, to sue. There is one course of action which no one can expect of a sane man: that is, solemnly to argue the points, to produce certificates from Saks and Harrods to say he has never, to the best of their belief, stolen a single article, to obtain testimonials signed by sixteen Fellows of the Royal Society, the Head of the Civil Service, a Lord Justice of Appeal and the Secretary of the M.C.C., testifying that they have known him for half a lifetime, and that even after a convivial evening they have not once seen him lurking in the vicinity of a tomb.

Such a reply is not on. It puts one in the same

psychological compartment as one's traducer. That is a condition from which one has a right to be excused.

The argument, fortunately, will suffer no loss if we ignore criticisms of this particular spirit, and any associated with them: for such intellectual contributions as they contain have been made, with civility and seriousness, by others.

There will need to be some cleaning up in due course. Textbook examples of the effects of some psychological states are not always conveniently come by: but a good many exist in this section of the literature. Do certain kinds of animosity lead to an inability to perform the physical act of reading? The evidence suggests so. The original lecture was quite short. The text is very simple. Most people, more particularly when attacking with virulence, would take pains to get straightforward quotations right. Yet this has not happened. There are various examples which, like the whole episode, seem to me somewhat bizarre. I will just select the crudest. One of my outrages in the Rede Lecture has been said to be the use of a phrase—'We die alone'. This phrase has been quoted and brandished, not only in a piece for which the publishers obtained my indemnification,[33] but in others which followed suit.[34] When I lost count, the number of times this quotation has been repeated was, I think, ten.

But where does the quotation come from? Cast your eye over the Rede Lecture with modest textual attentiveness. You will not find the phrase. It occurs nowhere. Indeed it would be surprising if it did. For I was trying to make a statement of the extremest singularity. No one would elect to make such a statement in plural form. Oddly enough, the English language does not meet the requirements comfortably. 'One dies alone' is not right. I finally had to use a phrase which was clumsy but said what I meant— Each of us dies alone'.

This concept, by the way, like so much else in the whole argument, is not original. It has been used in introspective thought, and particularly in intro-spective religious thought, for centuries. So far as I know, it was said first by Blaise Pascal: *On mourra seul.*

There will be scope for investigations of this kind later: but, I hope, not now. The important thing is to take the personalities, so far as we are able, out of the discussion. In what I am going to write myself I shall try to aim at this.

As I have already said, I think the most useful thing I can now do is to have another look at what I originally wrote: to look at it in the light of what has been said about it, for, against, and at right angles; and to do so with the help of new scientific, socio-logical and historical knowledge which, as research proceeds, should help, at least on a part of the problem, to provide not an opinion but an answer.

The statements in the lecture were as simple as I could make them. Any statements which have any reference to action must be simple. There is always something wrong, if one is straining to make the commonplace incomprehensible. I hedged the statements round with qualifications and I tried to illustrate some of them. I will now remove the qualifications and the pictures and rephrase the essence of the lecture as quietly as I can.

It is something like this. In our society (that is, advanced western society) we have lost even the pretence of a common culture. Persons educated with the greatest intensity we know can no longer communicate with each other on the plane of their major intellectual concern. This is serious for our creative, intellectual and, above all, our normal life. It is leading us to interpret the past wrongly, to misjudge the present, and to deny our hopes of the future. It is making it difficult or impossible for us to take good action.

I gave the most pointed example of this lack of communication in the shape of two groups of people, representing what I have christened 'the two cultures'. One of these contained the scientists, whose weight, achievement and influence did not need stressing. The other contained the literary intellectuals. I did not mean that literary intellectuals act as the main decision-makers of the western world. I meant that literary intellectuals represent, vocalise, and to some extent shape and predict the mood of the non-scientific culture: they do not make the decisions, but their words seep into the minds of those who do. Between these two groups—the scientists and the literary intellectuals—there is little communication and, instead of fellow-feeling, something like hostility.

This was intended as a description of, or a very crude first approximation to, our existing state of affairs. That it was a state of affairs I passionately disliked, I thought was made fairly clear. Curiously enough, some commentators have assumed that I approved of it; but at this I confess myself defeated, and take refuge in muttering Schiller's helpful line.[35]

To finish this précis. There is, of course, no complete solution. In the conditions of our age, or any age which we can foresee, Renaissance man is not possible. But we can do something. The chief means open to us is education—education mainly in primary and secondary schools, but also in colleges and universities. There is no excuse for letting another generation be as vastly ignorant, or as devoid of understanding and sympathy, as we are ourselves.

§ 3

From the beginning, the phrase 'the two cultures' evoked some protests. The word 'culture' or 'cultures' has been objected to: so, with much more substance,

has the number two. (No one, I think, has yet com-
plained about the definite article.)

I must have a word about these verbal points before
I come to the more wide-reaching arguments. The
term 'culture' in my title has two meanings, both of
which are precisely applicable to the theme. First,
'culture' has the sense of the dictionary definition,
'intellectual development, development of the mind'.
For many years this definition has carried overtones,
often of a deep and ambiguous sort. It happens that
few of us can help searching for a refined use of the
word: if anyone asks, What is culture? Who is
cultured? the needle points, by an extraordinary
coincidence, in the direction of ourselves.

But that, though a pleasing example of human
frailty, doesn't matter: what does matter is that any
refined definition, from Coleridge onwards, applies
at least as well (and also as imperfectly) to the development a scientist achieves *in the course of his professional
vocation* as to the 'traditional' mental development or
any of its offshoots. Coleridge said 'cultivation' where
we should say 'culture'—and qualified it as 'the
harmonious development of those qualities and
faculties which characterise our humanity'.[36] Well,
none of us manages that; in plain truth, either of our
cultures, whether literary or scientific, only deserves
the name of sub-culture. '*Qualities and faculties which
characterise our humanity.*' Curiosity about the natural
world, the use of symbolic systems of thought, are
two of the most precious and the most specifically

62

human of all human qualities. The traditional methods of mental development left them to be starved. So, in reverse, does scientific education starve our verbal faculties—the language of symbols is given splendid play, the language of words is not. On both sides we underestimate the spread of a human being's gifts.

But, if we are to use 'culture' in its refined sense at all, it is only lack of imagination, or possibly blank ignorance, which could deny it to scientists. There is no excuse for such ignorance. A whole body of literature has been built up over a generation, written, incidentally, in some of the most beautiful prose of our time, to demonstrate the intellectual, aesthetic and moral values inherent in the pursuit of science (compare A. N. Whitehead's *Science and the Modern World*, G. H. Hardy's *A Mathematician's Apology*, J. Bronowski's *Science and Human Values*). There are valuable insights scattered all over American and English writing of the last decade—Needham, Toulmin, Price, Piel, Newman, are only a few of the names that come to mind.

In the most lively of all contributions to this subject, a Third Programme feature not yet published, Bronowski deliberately avoided the word 'culture' for either side and chose as his title 'Dialogue between Two World Systems'. For myself, I believe the word is still appropriate and carries its proper meaning to sensible persons. But, while sticking to that word, I want to repeat what was intended to be my main message, but which has somehow got overlaid:

that neither the scientific system of mental development, nor the traditional, is adequate for our potentialities, for the work we have in front of us, for the world in which we ought to begin to live.

The word 'culture' has a second and technical meaning, which I pointed out explicitly in the original lecture. It is used by anthropologists to denote a group of persons living in the same environment, linked by common habits, common assumptions, a common way of life. Thus one talks of a Neanderthal culture, a La Tène culture, a Trobriand Island culture: the term, which is a very useful one, has been applied to groups within our own societies. For me this was a very strong additional reason for selecting the word; it isn't often one gets a word which can be used in two senses, both of which one explicitly intends. For scientists on the one side, literary intellectuals on the other, do in fact exist as cultures within the anthropological scope. There are, as I said before, common attitudes, common standards and patterns of behaviour, common approaches and assumptions. This does not mean that a person within a culture loses his individuality and free will. It does mean that, without knowing it, we are more than we think children of our time, place and training. Let me take two trivial and non-controversial examples. The overwhelming majority of the scientific culture (that is, the group of scientists observed through anthropological eyes) would feel certain, without needing to cogitate or examine their souls, that research was the primary function of a university. This attitude is automatic, it is part of their culture: but it would not be the attitude of such a proportion in the literary culture. On the other hand, the overwhelming majority of the literary culture would feel just as certain that not the slightest censorship of the printed word is, in any circumstances, permissible. This position doesn't have to be reached by individual thought: again it is part of the culture. It is such an unquestioned part, in fact, that the literary intellectuals have got their way more absolutely than, thirty years ago, would have seemed conceivable.

That is enough on 'cultures'. Now for the number Two. Whether this was the best choice, I am much less certain. Right from the start I introduced some qualifying doubts. I will repeat what I said, near the beginning of the lecture.

'The number 2 is a very dangerous number: that is why the dialectic is a dangerous process. Attempts to divide anything into two ought to be regarded with much suspicion. I have thought a long time about going in for further refinements: but in the end I have decided against. I was searching for something a little more than a dashing metaphor, a good deal less than a cultural map: and for those purposes the two cultures is about right, and subtilising any more would bring more disadvantages than it's worth.'

That still seems to me fairly sensible. But I am open to correction, and I have been much impressed by a new feature in the situation, which I will come to in a moment. Before that, however, I ought to mention two lines of argument; one goes happily away into nullity, the other, which I should once have followed myself, can be misleading. The first says, no, there aren't two cultures, there are a hundred and two, or two thousand and two, or any number you like to name. In a sense this is true: but it is also meaningless. Words are always simpler than the brute reality from which they make patterns: if they weren't, discussion and collective action would both be impossible. *Of course* there is sub-division after sub-division within, say, the scientific culture. Theoretical physicists tend to talk only to each other, and, like so many Cabots, to God. Either in scientific politics or open politics, organic chemists much more often than not turn out to be conservative: the reverse is true of biochemists. And so on. Hardy used to say that one could see all these diversities in action round the council table of the Royal Society. But Hardy, who was no respecter either of labels or institutions, would not on that account have said that the Royal Society represented nothing. In fact, its existence is a supreme manifestation or symbol of the scientific culture.[37] This attempt at excessive unsimplicity, the 'two thousand and two cultures' school of thought, crops up whenever anyone makes a proposal which opens up a prospect, however distant, of new action. It involves a skill which all conservative functionaries are masters of, as they

66

ingeniously protect the status quo: it is called 'the technique of the intricate defensive'.

The second line of argument draws, or attempts to draw, a clear line between pure science and technology (which is tending to become a pejorative word). This is a line that once I tried to draw myself:[38] but, though I can still see the reasons, I shouldn't now. The more I have seen of technologists at work, the more untenable the distinction has come to look. If you actually see someone design an aircraft, you find him going through the same experience— aesthetic, intellectual, moral—as though he were setting up an experiment in particle physics.

The scientific process has two motives: one is to understand the natural world, the other is to control it. Either of these motives may be dominant in any individual scientist; fields of science may draw their original impulses from one or the other. Cosmogony for example—the study of the origin and nature of the cosmos—is a pretty pure example of the first class. Medicine is the type specimen of the second. Yet, in all scientific fields, however the work originated, one motive becomes implicit in the other. From medicine, which is a classical technology, men have worked back to 'pure' scientific problems— such as, say, the structure of the haemoglobin molecule. From cosmogony, which seems the most unpractical of all subjects, have come insights into nuclear fission—which, for evil and potentially for good, no one could call an unpractical activity.

This complex dialectic between pure and applied science is one of the deepest problems in scientific history. At present there is much of it which we don't begin to understand. Sometimes the practical need which inspires a wave of invention is brutally obvious. No one has to be told why British, American, German scientists suddenly—at first unknown to each other—made great advances in electronics between 1935 and 1945. It was equally plain that this immensely powerful technological weapon would soon be used in the purest of scientific researches, from astronomy to cybernetics. But what conceivable external stimulus or social correlative set Bolyai, Gauss and Lobachewski—also, in the beginning, unknown to each other—working at the same point in time on non-Euclidean geometry, apparently one of the most abstract of all fields of the conceptual imagination? It is going to be difficult to find a satisfying answer. But we may make it impossible, if we start by assuming a difference in kind between pure science and applied.

§ 4

So the phrase 'the two cultures' still seems appropriate for the purpose I had in mind. I now think, however, that I should have stressed more heavily that I was speaking as an Englishman, from experience drawn mainly from English society. I did in fact say this, and I said also that this cultural divide seems at its sharpest in England. I now realise that I did not emphasise it enough.

In the United States, for example, the divide is nothing like so unbridgeable. There are pockets of the literary culture, influenced by the similar culture in England, which are as extreme in resisting communication and in ceasing to communicate: but that isn't generally true over the literary culture as a whole, much less over the entire intellectual society. And, just because the divide is not so deep, just because the situation is not accepted as a fact of life, far more active steps are being taken to improve it. This is an interesting example of one of the laws of social change: change doesn't happen when things are at their worst, but when they are looking up. So it is at Yale and Princeton and Michigan and California, that scientists of world standing are talking to non-specialised classes: at M.I.T. and Cal. Tech. where students of the sciences are receiving a serious humane education. In the last few years, all over the country, a visitor cannot help being astonished by the resilience and inventiveness of American higher education—ruefully so, if he happens to be an Englishman.[39]

I think also that writing as an Englishman made me insensitive to something which may, within a few years, propel the argument in another direction or which conceivably may already have started to do just that. I have been increasingly impressed by a body of intellectual opinion, forming itself, without organisation, without any kind of lead or conscious direction, under the surface of this debate. This is the new feature I referred to a little earlier. This body of opinion seems to come from intellectual persons in a variety of fields—social history, sociology, demography, political science, economics, government (in the American academic sense), psychology, medicine, and social arts such as architecture. It seems a mixed bag: but there is an inner consistency. All of them are concerned with how human beings are living or have lived—and concerned, not in terms of legend, but of fact. I am not implying that they agree with each other, but in their approach to cardinal problems—such as the human effects of the scientific revolution, which is the fighting point of this whole affair—they display, at the least, a family resemblance.

I ought, I see now, to have expected this. I haven't much excuse for not doing so. I have been in close intellectual contact with social historians most of my life: they have influenced me a good deal: their recent researches were the basis for a good many of my statements. But nevertheless I was slow to observe the development of what, in the terms of our formulae, is becoming something like a third culture. I might have been quicker if I had not been the prisoner of my English upbringing, conditioned to be suspicious of any but the established intellectual disciplines, unreservedly at home only with the 'hard' subjects. For this I am sorry.

It is probably too early to speak of a third culture

already in existence. But I am now convinced that this is coming. When it comes, some of the difficulties of communication will at last be softened: for such a culture has, just to do its job, to be on speaking terms with the scientific one. Then, as I said, the focus of this argument will be shifted, in a direction which will be more profitable to us all.

There are signs that this is happening. Some social historians, as well as being on speaking terms with scientists, have felt bound to turn their attention to the literary intellectuals, or more exactly to some manifestations of the literary culture at its extreme. Concepts such as the 'organic community' or the nature of pre-industrial society or the scientific revolution are being dealt with, under the illumination of the knowledge of the last ten years. These new examinations are of great importance for our intellectual and moral health.

Since they touch on the parts of my lecture on which I have the deepest feelings, I shall revert to them once again in the next section. After that I shall leave them in the hands of those professionally qualified to speak.

One word about another passage where I showed bad judgment. In my account of the lack of communication between the two cultures, I didn't exaggerate: if anything I understated the case, as has been proved by subsequent pieces of fieldwork.[40] Yet I have regretted that I used as my test question about scientific literacy, *What do you know of the*

Second Law of Thermodynamics? It is, in fact, a good question. Many physical scientists would agree that it is perhaps the most pointed question. This law is one of the greatest depth and generality: it has its own sombre beauty: like all the major scientific laws, it evokes reverence. There is, of course, no value in a non-scientist just knowing it by the rubric in an encyclopedia. It needs understanding, which can't be attained unless one has learnt some of the language of physics. That understanding ought to be part of a common twentieth-century culture—as Lord Cherwell once said, more astringently than I have done, in the House of Lords. Nevertheless I wish that I had chosen a different example. I had forgotten—like a playwright who has lost touch with his audience— that the law is called by what to most people is an unfamiliar, and therefore a funny, name. To be honest, I had forgotten how funny the unfamiliar is—I ought to have remembered the jocularity with which the English greeted the Russian patronymics in Chekhov, roaring their heads off each time they heard Fyodor Ilyich or Lyubov Andreievna, expressing their blissful ignorance of a formal nomenclature both more courteous and more human than their own.

So I got a laugh: but again, like an incompetent playwright, I got a laugh in the wrong place. I should now treat the matter differently, and I should put forward a branch of science which ought to be a requisite in the common culture, certainly for anyone now at school. This branch of science at present goes by the name of molecular biology. Is that funny? I think that possibly it is already well enough domesticated. Through a whole set of lucky chances, this study is ideally suited to fit into a new model of education. It is fairly self-contained. It begins with the analysis of crystal structure, itself a subject aesthetically beautiful and easily comprehended. It goes on to the application of these methods to molecules which have literally a vital part in our own existence—molecules of proteins, nucleic acids: molecules immensely large (by molecular standards) and which turn out to be of curious shapes, for nature, when interested in what we call life, appears to have a taste for the rococo. It includes the leap of genius by which Crick and Watson snatched at the structure of DNA and so taught us the essential lesson about our genetic inheritance.

Unlike thermodynamics, the subject does not involve serious conceptual difficulties. In fact, in terms of concept, it doesn't reach so deep, and it is for other reasons that it has a first claim upon us. It needs very little mathematics to understand. There are few parts of the hard sciences of which one can understand so much without mathematical training. What one needs most of all is a visual and three-dimensional imagination, and it is a study where painters and sculptors could be instantaneously at home.

It exemplifies, with extreme neatness, some of the characteristics of the whole scientific culture, its subdivisions and its community. Exponents of the 'two thousand and two cultures' school of thought will be glad to hear that only a handful of people in the world—five hundred?—would be competent to follow in detail each step of the process by which, say, Perutz and Kendrew finally disentangled the structure of the haem proteins. After all, Perutz was at haemoglobin, on and off, for twenty-five years. But any scientist with the patience to learn could get instructed in those processes, and any scientist knows it. The great majority of scientists can acquire an adequate working knowledge of what the results mean. All scientists without exception accept the results. It is a nice demonstration of the scientific culture at work.

I have said that the ideas in this branch of science are not as physically deep, or of such universal physical significance, as those in the Second Law. That is true. The Second Law is a generalisation which covers the cosmos. This new study deals only with microscopic parts of the cosmos, which may—no one knows—exist only on this earth: but since those microscopic parts happen to be connected with biological life, they are of importance to each of us. It is very hard to write about this importance. It is better, I think, to take a self-denying ordinance and let the researches of the next ten years make it plain. But here is a statement which is not seriously controversial. This branch of science is likely to affect the way in which *men think of themselves* more profoundly than any scientific advance since Darwin's—and probably more so than Darwin's.

That seems a sufficient reason why the next generation should learn about it. The Church recognises invincible ignorance: but here the ignorance is not, or need not be, invincible. This study could be grafted into any of our educational systems, at high school or college levels, without artificiality and without strain. I dare say that, as usual, this is an idea which is already floating around the world, and that, as I write this paragraph, some American college has already laid on the first course.

§ 5

Major scientific breakthroughs, and in particular those as closely connected to human flesh and bone as this one in molecular biology, or even more, another which we may expect in the nature of the higher nervous system, are bound to touch both our hopes and our resignations. That is: ever since men began to think introspectively about themselves, they have made guesses, and sometimes had profound intuitions, about those parts of their own nature which seemed to be predestined. It is possible that within a generation some of these guesses will have been tested against exact knowledge. No one can predict what such an intellectual revolution will mean: but I believe that one of the consequences will be to make us feel not less but more responsible towards our brother men.

It was for this reason among others that, in the original lecture, I drew a distinction between the individual condition and the social condition. In doing so, I stressed the solitariness, the ultimate tragedy, at the core of each individual life; and this has worried a good many who found the rest of the statement acceptable. It is very hard, of course, to subdue the obsessions of one's own temperament; this specific note creeps into a good deal of what I have written, as Alfred Kazin has shrewdly pointed out:[41] it is not an accident that my novel sequence is called *Strangers and Brothers*. Nevertheless, this distinction, however it is drawn, is imperative, unless we are going to sink into the facile social pessimism of our time, unless we are going to settle into our own egocentric chill.

So I will try to make the statement without much emphasis of my own. We should most of us agree, I think, that in the individual life of each of us there is much that, in the long run, one cannot do anything about. Death is a fact—one's own death, the deaths of those one loves. There is much that makes one suffer which is irremediable: one struggles against it all the way, but there is an irremediable residue left. These are facts: they will remain facts as long as man remains man. This is part of the individual condition: call it tragic, comic, absurd, or, like some of the best and bravest of people, shrug it off.

But it isn't all. One looks outside oneself to other lives, to which one is bound by love, affection, loyalty, obligation: each of those lives has the same irremediable components as one's own; but there are also components that one can help, or that can give one help. It is in this tiny extension of the personality, it is in this seizing on the possibilities of hope, that we become more fully human: it is a way to improve the quality of one's life: it is, for oneself, the beginning of the social condition.

Finally, one can try to understand the condition of lives, not close to one's own, which one cannot know face to face. Each of these lives—that is, the lives of one's fellow human beings—again has limits of irremediability like one's own. Each of them has needs, some of which can be met: the totality of all is the social condition.

We cannot know as much as we should about the social condition all over the world. But we can know, we do know, two most important things. First we can meet the harsh facts of the flesh, on the level where all of us are, or should be, one. We know that the vast majority, perhaps two-thirds, of our fellow men are living in the immediate presence of illness and premature death; their expectation of life is half of ours, most are under-nourished, many are near to starving, many starve. Each of these lives is afflicted by suffering, different from that which is intrinsic in the individual condition. But this suffering is unnecessary and can be lifted. This is the second important thing which we know—or, if we don't know it, there is no excuse or absolution for us.

We cannot avoid the realisation that applied science has made it possible to remove unnecessary suffering from a billion individual human lives—to remove suffering of a kind, which, in our own privileged society, we have largely forgotten, suffering so elementary that it is not genteel to mention it. For example, we *know* how to heal many of the sick: to prevent children dying in infancy and mothers in childbirth: to produce enough food to alleviate hunger: to throw up a minimum of shelter: to ensure that there aren't so many births that our other efforts are in vain. All this we *know* how to do.

It does not require one additional scientific discovery, though new scientific discoveries must help us. It depends on the spread of the scientific revolution all over the world. There is no other way. For most human beings, this is the point of hope. It will certainly happen. It may take longer than the poor will peacefully accept. How long it takes, and the fashion in which it is done, will be a reflex of the quality of our lives, especially of the lives of those of us born lucky: as most in the western world were born.[42] When it is achieved, then our consciences will be a little cleaner; and those coming after us will at least be able to think that the elemental needs of others aren't a daily reproach to any sentient person, that for the first time some genuine dignity has come upon us all.

Man doesn't live by bread alone—yes, that has been said often enough in the course of these discussions.

It has been said occasionally with a lack of imagination, a provincialism, that makes the mind boggle: for it is not a remark that one of us in the western world can casually address to most Asians, to most of our fellow human beings, in the world as it now exists. But we can, we should, say it to ourselves. For we know how, once the elemental needs are satisfied, we do not find it easy to do something worthy and satisfying with our lives. Probably it will never be easy. Conceivably men in the future, if they are as lucky as we are now, will struggle with our existential discontents, or new ones of their own. They may, like some of us, try—through sex or drink or drugs—to intensify the sensational life. Or they may try to improve the quality of their lives, through an extension of their responsibilities, a deepening of the affections and the spirit, in a fashion which, though we can aim at it for ourselves and our own societies, we can only dimly perceive.

But, though our perception may be dim, it isn't dim enough to obscure one truth: that one mustn't despise the elemental needs, when one has been granted them and others have not. To do so is not to display one's superior spirituality. It is simply to be inhuman, or more exactly anti-human.

Here, in fact, was what I intended to be the centre of the whole argument. Before I wrote the lecture I thought of calling it 'The Rich and the Poor', and I rather wish that I hadn't changed my mind.

The scientific revolution is the only method by

which most people can gain the primal things (years of life, freedom from hunger, survival for children)—the primal things which we take for granted and which have in reality come to us through having had our own scientific revolution not so long ago. Most people want these primal things. Most people, wherever they are being given a chance, are rushing into the scientific revolution.

To misunderstand this position is to misunderstand both the present and the future. It simmers beneath the surface of world politics. Though the form of politics may look the same, its content is being altered as the scientific revolution pours in. We have not been as quick as we should to draw the right consequences, very largely because of the division of the cultures. It has been hard for politicians and administrators to grasp the practical truth of what scientists were telling them. But now it is beginning to be accepted. It is often accepted most easily by men of affairs, whatever their political sympathies, engineers, or priests, or doctors, all those who have a strong comradely physical sympathy for other humans. If others can get the primal things—yes, that is beyond argument; that is simply good.

Curiously enough, there are many who would call themselves liberals and yet who are antipathetic to this change. Almost as though sleepwalking they drift into an attitude which, to the poor of the world, is a denial of all human hope. This attitude, which misinterprets both the present and the future, seems to be connected with a similar misinterpretation of the past. It is on this point that representatives of the putative third culture have been speaking with trenchancy.

The argument is about the first wave of the scientific revolution, the transformation which we call the industrial revolution, and it is occupied with questions about what, in the most elementary human terms, life was like in pre-industrial as compared with industrial society. We can gain some insights, of course, from the present world, which is a vast sociological laboratory in which one can observe all kinds of society from the neolithic to the advanced industrial. We are also now accumulating substantial evidence of our own past.

When I made some remarks about the industrial revolution, I had imagined that the findings of recent research in social history were better known. Otherwise I should have documented what I said: but that seemed like documenting a platitude. Did anyone think that, in the primal terms in which I have just been discussing the poor countries of the present world, our ancestors' condition was so very different? Or that the industrial revolution had not brought us in three or four generations to a state entirely new in the harsh, unrecorded continuity of poor men's lives? I couldn't believe it. I knew, of course, the force of nostalgia, myth, and plain snobbery. In all families, at all times, there are stories of blessed existences, just before one's childhood: there were in my own.

Myth—I ought to have remembered what Malinowski taught us, that people believe their myths as fact. I certainly ought to have remembered that, when anyone is asked what he would have been in a previous incarnation, he nominates—if he is modest—something like a Jacobean cleric or an eighteenth-century squire. He wouldn't have been any such thing. The overwhelming probability is that he would have been a peasant. If we want to talk about our ancestors, that is whence we came.

I was at fault, I suppose, in not trying to be more persuasive against these kinds of resistance. Anyway, there is no need for me to say much more. There are plenty of scholars professionally concerned with pre-industrial social history. Now we know something of the elemental facts of the lives and deaths of peasants and agricultural labourers in seventeenth- and eighteenth-century England and France. They are not comfortable facts. J. H. Plumb, in one of his attacks on the teaching of a pretty-pretty past, has written: 'No one in his senses would choose to have been born in a previous age unless he could be certain that he would have been born into a prosperous family, that he would have enjoyed extremely good health, and that he could have accepted stoically the death of the majority of his children.'

It is worth anyone's while—in fact no one ought to escape the experience—to study the results which the French demographers have obtained in the last decade. In the seventeenth and eighteenth centuries, parish registers in France were kept with great accuracy, much more commonly so than in England —births, marriages and deaths the only tiny records, the only traces, of so many human lives. These records are now being analysed all over France.[43] They tell a story which can be duplicated in Asian (or Latin American) communities today.

In the dry but appallingly eloquent language of statistics, the historians explain to us that, in eighteenth-century French villages, the median age of marriage was higher than the median age of death. The *average* length of life was perhaps a third of ours, and appreciably less, because of the deaths in childbirth, for women than for men (*it is only quite recently, and in lucky countries, that women, on the average, have had a chance of living as long as men*). The greater part of entire communities[44] died of starvation, which appears to have been a common occurrence.

Though English records are nothing like so complete, Peter Laslett and his collaborators have discovered some late seventeenth-century registers,[45] and are actively extending their researches. The same stark conclusions stand out—except that in England there is as yet no proof of periodical famine, though it was endemic among the Scottish poor.

There is a mass of other evidence, from many kinds of provenance, all pointing in the same direction. In the light of it, no one should feel it seriously possible to talk about a pre-industrial Eden, from which our ancestors were, by the wicked machinations of applied science, brutally expelled. When and where was this Eden? Will someone who hankers after the myth tell us where he believes it was located, not in terms of wishful fancy, but in place and time, in historical and geographical fact? Then the social historians can examine the case and there can be a respectable discussion.

The present position is not respectable. One can't talk or teach false social history when the professionals are proving the falsity under one's eyes. Yet, as Plumb has publicly protested, what he calls 'this nonsense' is being taught. To anyone educated in an exact discipline it all seems very peculiar, almost as though reading itself had gone out of fashion as an activity, certainly the reading of any evidence which contradicts the stereotypes of fifty years ago. It is rather as though the teachers of physics had ignored the quantum theory and had gone on, year after year, teaching precisely those radiation laws which the quantum theory had been brought in to replace. And teaching them with that special insistence which strains the voices of priests of a dying religion.

It is important for the pre-industrial believers to confront the social historians. Then we can get a basis of fact accepted. One can teach a myth: but when the myth is seen as fact, and when the fact is disproved, the myth becomes a lie. No one can teach a lie.

I have restricted myself to primal things. It seems to me better that people should live rather than die:

that they shouldn't be hungry: that they shouldn't have to watch their children die. Here, if anywhere, we are members one of another. If we are not members one of another, if we have no sympathy at this elemental level, then we have no human concern at all, and any pretence of a higher kind of sympathy is a mockery. Fortunately most of us are not so affectless as that.

Anyone who has had a physical misfortune knows that many acquaintances who would feel for him in no other circumstances, genuinely feel for him in this one. The sympathy is visceral: it is a sign that we cannot deny our common humanity.

Therefore the social condition is with us, we are part of it, we cannot deny it. Millions of individual lives, in some lucky countries like our own, have, by one gigantic convulsion of applied science over the last hundred and fifty years, been granted some share of the primal things. Billions of individual lives, over the rest of the world, will be granted or will seize the same. This is the indication of time's arrow. It is by far the greatest revolution our kind has known. We have been living through rapid change for three or four generations. Now the change is going faster. It is bound to go a great deal faster still. This is the condition in which we are both agents and spectators. Our response to it affects, and often determines, what we like and dislike in our world, what action we take, the nature of the art we value or practise, the nature of our appreciation of science. It determines also, I fancy, the way in which some straightforward proposals about education, intended to be simple and practical, have been made the jumping-off point for a debate on first and last things.

§ 6

We are only just beginning to live with the industrial-scientific revolution; we have taken the first positive steps to control it, to compensate for its losses as well as to absorb its gains. The modern industrial communities of, say, Northern Italy or Sweden, are qualitatively different from those which first accumulated in Lancashire or New England. The whole process has not yet dived into our imaginative understanding. We who comment about it stand outside: socially in that most dangerous of positions, one tiny step more privileged than those who are taking part.

One point, however, is clear; those who are taking part have never paid one instant's attention to the lookers-on who would like them to reject industrial-isation. As I said in the original lecture, this is a manifest fact in all societies all over the world. It is these witnesses whom we ought to consult, not those of us who are one step luckier, who think we know what is good for them.

The primary reason for their enthusiasm, which was set out in the last section, was so strong that men would need no others. But I believe there are others, quite deep in the individual's intuitive life, which impel most young people to elect for living in towns whenever they have a free choice, and others again which impel nearly all unprivileged people to prefer a highly organised society to one based on simple power relations.

The first class of reasons is obvious enough, and does not need explication: have you ever been young? The second is a little more subtle. Perhaps I can illustrate it by, so to speak, an example in reverse. I am reminded of D. H. Lawrence[46] reflecting on an anecdote in Dana's *Two Years Before the Mast*. The passage is a very long one, and should be read in full: it is about Dana feeling revolted when the captain of the ship has a sailor called Sam flogged. Lawrence denounces Dana for being revolted: Lawrence approves.

Master and servant—or master and man relationship is, essentially, a polarized flow, like love. It is a circuit of vitalism which flows between master and man and forms a very precious nourishment to each, and keeps both in a state of subtle, quivering, vital equilibrium. Deny it as you like, it is so. But once you *abstract* both master and man, and make them both serve an *idea*: production, wage, efficiency, and so on: so that each looks on himself as an instrument performing a certain repeated evolution, then you have changed the vital, quivering circuit of master and man into a mechanical machine unison. Just another way of life: or anti-life.

· · · · · · · · ·

Flogging.

You have a Sam, a fat slow fellow, who has got slower and more slovenly as the weeks wear on. You have a master who has grown more irritable in his authority. Till Sam becomes simply wallowing in his slackness, makes your gorge rise. And the master is on red hot iron.

Now these two men, Captain and Sam, are there in a very unsteady equilibrium of command and obedience. A polarized flow. Definitely polarized.

.   .   .   .

'Tie up that lousy swine!' roars the enraged Captain.

And whack! Whack! down on the bare back of that sloucher Sam comes the cat.

What does it do? By Jove, it goes like ice-cold water into his spine. Down those lashes runs the current of the Captain's rage, right into the blood and into the toneless ganglia of Sam's voluntary system. Crash! Crash! runs the lightning flame, right into the cores of the living nerves.

And the living nerves respond. They start to vibrate. They brace up. The blood begins to go quicker. The nerves begin to recover their vividness. It is their tonic. The man Sam has a new clear day of intelligence, and a smarty back. The Captain has a new relief, a new ease in his authority, and a sore heart.

There is a new equilibrium, and a fresh start. The *physical* intelligence of a Sam is restored, the turgidity is relieved from the veins of the Captain.

It is a natural form of human coition, interchange.

It is good for Sam to be flogged. It is good, on this occasion, for the Captain to have Sam flogged. I say so.

This reflection is the exact opposite of that which would occur to anyone who had never held, or expected to hold, the right end of the whip—which means most of the poor of the world, all the unprivileged, the teeming majority of our fellow men. Such a man may not be lazy like Sam: nevertheless he doesn't like being in another's power. He doesn't take this Rousseauish view of the virtue of the direct expression of emotion, or 'the circuit of vitalism',[47] or 'the blood contact of life'. *He* has suffered others' tempers, at the receiving end. *He* is not romantic at all about the beauties of the master-and-man relation: that illusion is open only to those who have climbed one step up and are hanging on by their fingernails. *He* knows, through the long experience of the poor, what the real condition of direct power is like—if you want it treated with ultimate humanity and wisdom read Bruno Bettelheim's *The Informed Heart*.

So, with singular unanimity the unprivileged have elected for societies where they are as far away as possible from the Captain-Sam situation—which, of course, highly articulated societies are. Trade unions, collective dealing, the entire apparatus of modern industry—they may be maddening to those who have never had the experience of the poor, but they stand like barbed wire against the immediate assertion of the individual will. And, as soon as the poor began to escape from their helplessness, the assertion of the individual will was the first thing they refused to take.

With the scientific revolution going on around us, what has our literature made of it? This is a topic which I mentioned in the lecture, but about which almost everything remains to be said. Probably some sort of examination will be produced in the next few years. For myself, I shall be glad to get this part of the controversy into better perspective. I will make one or two comments to show some of my present thinking: to those, if I believe I can add something useful, I shall in due course return.

Let me begin some distance off the point. It happens that, of all novelists, Dostoevsky is the one I know the best. When I was twenty, I thought *The Brothers Karamazov* was by a long way the greatest novel ever written, and its author the most magnificent of novelists. Gradually my enthusiasm became more qualified: as I grew older I found Tolstoy meaning more to me. But Dostoevsky is to this day one of the novelists I most admire: besides Tolstoy there seem to me only two or three others who can live in the same light.

This confession of personal taste is not so irrelevant as it seems. Of the great novelists Dostoevsky is the one whose social attitudes are most explicitly revealed —not in his novels, where he is ambiguous, but in the *Writer's Diary* which he published once a month during the years 1876–80, when he was in his fifties and near the peak of his fame. In the *Diary*, which was produced as a single-handed effort, he gave answers to readers' problems of the heart (the advice was almost always practical and wise), but he devoted most of his space to political propaganda, to passionate and increasingly unambiguous expression of his own prescripts for action.

They are pretty horrifying, even after ninety years. He was virulently anti-semitic: he prayed for war: he was against any kind of emancipation at any time; he was a fanatical supporter of the autocracy, and an equally fanatical opponent of any improvement in the lives of the common people (on the grounds that they loved their suffering and were ennobled by it). He was in fact the supreme reactionary: other writers since have aspired to this condition, but no one has had his force of nature and his psychological complexity. It is worth noting that he wasn't speaking in a vacuum; this wasn't like Lawrence banging away with exhortations, some of them similarly regrettable.[48] Dostoevsky lived in society; his diary was influential, and acted as the voice of the ultra-conservatives, to whom he himself in secret acted as a kind of psychological adviser.

Thus I have not a social idea in common with him. If I had been his contemporary, he would have tried to get me put in gaol. And yet I know him to be a great writer, and I know that, not with detached admiration, but with a feeling much warmer. So do present day Russians know it. Their response is much the same as mine. Posterity is in the long run forgiving, if a writer is good enough.[49] No one could call Dostoevsky an agreeable character, and he did finite harm. But compare him with the generous and open-hearted Chernyshevsky, who had a sense of the future of the world flat contrary to Dostoevsky's, and whose foresight has turned out nearer to the truth. The goodwill, the social passion of Chernyshevsky have kept his memory fresh: but posterity ignores wrong or wicked judgments, and it is Dostoevsky's books which stay alive. *What is to be done?* or *The Brothers Karamazov*?—posterity, if it knows anything of the two personal histories, gives a grim, reluctant, sarcastic smile, and knows which it has to choose.

It will be the same in the future. Persons ignorant of the nature of change, antagonistic to the scientific revolution which will impose social changes such as none of us can foresee, often think and talk and hope as though all literary judgments for ever will be made from the same viewpoint as that of contemporary London or New York: as though we had reached a kind of social plateau which is the final resting-ground of literate man. That, of course, is absurd. The social matrix will change, education will change, with greater acceleration than it did between the time of the *Edinburgh Review* and the *Partisan Review*: judgments will change. But it is not necessary to go to extremes of subjectivity. Major writers are able to survive the invention of new categories; they resist the influence of ideologies, including most of all their own. As we read, our imaginations stretch wider than our beliefs. If we construct mental boxes to shut out what won't fit, then we make ourselves meaner.[50] Among near contemporaries whom I admire, I could mention Bernard Malamud, Robert Graves, William Golding: it would be a tough job to assimilate these three into any scheme or ideology, literary or non-literary, which could conceivably be associated with me. So, in a future society, different from ours, some of the great literary names of our time will still be venerated. This will be true of the major talents in the 'movement' of which Dostoevsky was a distant and eccentric precursor and which lasted, as the literature of the western *avant-garde*, down until the very recent past.

The writers who have taken part in this movement are nowadays often called 'modernists' or 'moderns'; the terms may seem a little odd for a school which began well back in the nineteenth century and which has left scarcely any active practitioners; but literary terms are odd, and if we don't like these we can think of them as terms of art, like the adjectives in New College or *art nouveau*. Anyway, we all know what is meant: there would be fair agreement on some of the representative names—Laforgue, Henry James, Dujardin, Dorothy Richardson, T. S. Eliot, Yeats, Pound, Hulme, Joyce, Lawrence, Sologub, Andrei Bely,[51] Virginia Woolf, Wyndham Lewis, Gide, Musil, Kafka, Benn, Valéry, Faulkner, Beckett.

According to taste, and according to one's fundamental attitude to the implications of modernism, one

93

adds names or subtracts them.[52] Thus Lukács, by far the most powerful of its antagonists, would not include Thomas Mann: while Trilling, one of its committed defenders, certainly would. And so on.

We should nearly all agree that the modernist movement includes a majority, though not all, of the high talents in western literature over a longish period. We should further agree that the individual works of individual writers have an existence of their own; and that the greatest of the modernists' creations will, like Dostoevsky's, swim above the underswell of argument in a changing culture. But about what the movement means in social terms (that is, the social roots from which it grew and its effects upon society), its meaning in the here-and-now of our divided culture, and its influence in the future—here there is a disagreement which can't be glossed over and which may continue after most of us are dead.

There have recently appeared three interesting texts: Lionel Trilling's *The Modern Element in Modern Literature*,[53] Stephen Spender's *The Struggle of the Modern*,[54] Georg Lukács's *The Meaning of Contemporary Realism*.[55] The first striking thing is that, when they are talking of modernism and modern literature, they are talking of what is recognisably the same thing. They value it differently: their formal analysis is different: but, behind all that, the essence to which they are responding is the same.

The confrontation of Lukács and Trilling is picturesque. Each is a very clever man, and clever in somewhat the same fashion. Each brings by design to literary criticism a range of equipment from non-literary disciplines: Lukács from philosophy and economics, Trilling from Freudian psychology. They often give the common impression of being unempirical: when they try to be empirical they have a tendency to overdo it. On modernism, Lukács is temperately and courteously anti, Trilling devotedly pro. In a long and sustained analysis of modernism, Lukács sees its characteristic features as rejection of narrative objectivity: dissolution of the personality: ahistoricity: static view of the human condition (meaning by this mainly what I have called the social condition).

Trilling's views are familiar to most of us. In his recent essay there is an explicit passage:

The author of *The Magic Mountain* once said that all his work could be understood as an effort to free himself from the middle class and this, of course, will serve to describe the intention of all modern literature . . . the end is not freedom from the middle class but freedom from society itself. I venture to say that the idea of losing oneself up to the point of self-destruction, of surrendering oneself to experience without regard to self-interest or morality, escaping wholly from the societal bonds, is an 'element' somewhere in the mind of every modern person who dares to think of what Arnold in his unaffected Victorian way called the 'fullness of spiritual perfection'.

Reading these closely argued, deeply felt and often moving essays one after the other, that is, Lukács's and

Trilling's, one has a curious sense of *déjà vu*. Aren't the two insights, which look so different, seeing the same phenomenon? One approves, the other disapproves, and yet there is a link. They might disagree about the social causes of modernism—but each is too subtle to think that these are simple. As Harry Levin has demonstrated,[56] the social origins of classical nineteenth-century realism are more complex than we used to think.

Lukács and Trilling are describing what has happened. The descriptions under the surface often run together. For Trilling's 'freedom from society' presupposes a static view of society. It is the romantic conception of the artist carried to its extreme. And the romantic conception of the artist only has full meaning if there is a social cushion, unaffected by change, unaffected by the scientific revolution, to fall back on. Such an attitude, such a desire, can lead to turning the original dichotomy on its head and taking an optimistic view of one's individual condition and a pessimistic view of the social one. Trilling would not do this, of course: he is too serious a man. But it is a temptation characteristic of the worst-spirited of modernist literature.

I find myself asking a question. It is not a rhetorical question, and I don't know the answer. It would be a satisfaction to know it. The question is this: how far is it possible to share the hopes of the scientific revolution, the modest difficult hopes for other human lives, and at the same time participate without qualification in the kind of literature which has just been defined?

§ 8

Finally, it has been said of the original lecture that it is oblivious of politics. At first sight, this seems strange; for I have written, both in novels and essays, more about politics, in particular 'closed' politics (that is, the way decisions are really taken in power-groups, as contrasted with the way they are supposed to be taken), than most people of our time. But in fact this species of criticism is not as strange as it seems; for those who have uttered it mean something a good deal different from what the overt words convey. That is, they mean by 'politics' something more limited than most of us can accept, and something which is, in my view, profoundly dangerous. They mean, to be brutal, by 'politics' the waging of the cold war. Their criticism amounts to saying that I did not relate the lecture to the cold war, as it was being waged in 1959: or, more sinister still, that I did not accept the cold war as the prime absolute of our age, and of all ages to come.

Of course I didn't. Not in 1959, nor for a good many years before that. It seemed to me that nearly every indication, human, economic, above all technological, pointed the other way. If one knew a little about military technology, it was likely, oddly enough, not only to make the dangers appear sharper, but also the possibility of hope: for it was fairly clear that the discontinuities in military technology could not possibly leave the cold war untouched for long. It was *that* kind of politics, simmering under the surface of the open formulations with which I was concerned, and on the strength of which I made judgments which were totally unlike those of my critics. Some of mine were wrong: in the Rede Lecture I much over-estimated the speed of Chinese industrialisation. But the more significant ones, now that time has passed and we can check some of our guesses, I see no reason to change.

This leads me to the major theme of what I set out to say. Let me try again to make myself clear. It is dangerous to have two cultures which can't or don't communicate. In a time when science is determining much of our destiny, that is, whether we live or die, it is dangerous in the most practical terms. Scientists can give bad advice[57] and decision-makers can't know whether it is good or bad. On the other hand, scientists in a divided culture provide a knowledge of some potentialities which is theirs alone. All this makes the political process more complex, and in some ways more dangerous, than we should be prepared to tolerate for long, either for the purposes of avoiding disasters, or for fulfilling—what is waiting as a challenge to our conscience and goodwill—a definable social hope.

At present we are making do in our half-educated

fashion, struggling to hear messages, obviously of great importance, as though listening to a foreign language in which one only knows a few words. Sometimes, and perhaps often, the logic of applied science is modifying or shaping the political process itself. This has happened over nuclear tests, where we have been lucky enough to see, what hasn't been common in our time, a triumph for human sense. The triumph might have come sooner, if the logic of applied science had been as much at educated persons' disposal as the logic of language. But still, let's not minimise our triumphs. The worst doesn't always happen, as a friend said to me in the summer of 1940. I am beginning to believe that we shall escape or circumvent the greater dangers with which science has confronted us. If I wrote the lecture again now, there would still be anxiety in it, but less dread.

Escaping the dangers of applied science is one thing. Doing the simple and manifest good which applied science has put in our power is another, more difficult, more demanding of human qualities, and in the long run far more enriching to us all. It will need energy, self-knowledge, new skills. It will need new perceptions into both closed and open politics.

In the original lecture, as now, I was isolating only one small corner of the situation: I was talking primarily to educators and those being educated, about something which we all understand and which is within our grasp. Changes in education will not, by themselves, solve our problems: but without those changes we shan't even realise what the problems are.

Changes in education are not going to produce miracles. The division of our culture is making us more obtuse than we need be: we can repair communications to some extent: but, as I have said before, we are not going to turn out men and women who understand as much of our world as Piero della Francesca did of his, or Pascal, or Goethe. With good fortune, however, we can educate a large proportion of our better minds so that they are not ignorant of imaginative experience, both in the arts and in science, nor ignorant either of the endowments of applied science, of the remediable suffering of most of their fellow humans, and of the responsibilities which, once they are seen, cannot be denied.

NOTES

1 'The Two Cultures', *New Statesman*, 6 October 1956.

2 This lecture was delivered to a Cambridge audience, and so I used some points of reference which I did not need to explain. G. H. Hardy, 1877–1947, was one of the most distinguished pure mathematicians of his time, and a picturesque figure in Cambridge both as a young don and on his return in 1931 to the Sadleirian Chair of Mathematics.

3 I said a little more about this connection in *The Times Literary Supplement*, 'Challenge to the Intellect', 15 August 1958. I hope some day to carry the analysis further.

4 It would be more accurate to say that, for literary reasons, we felt the prevailing literary modes were useless to us. We were, however, reinforced in that feeling when it occurred to us that those prevailing modes went hand in hand with social attitudes either wicked, or absurd, or both.

5 An analysis of the schools from which Fellows of the Royal Society come tells its own story. The distribution is markedly different from that of, for example, members of the Foreign Service or Queen's Counsel.

6 Compare George Orwell's *1984*, which is the strongest possible wish that the future should not exist, with J. D. Bernal's *World Without War*.

7 *Subjective*, in contemporary technological jargon, means 'divided according to subjects'. *Objective* means 'directed towards an object'. *Philosophy* means

'general intellectual approach or attitude' (for example, a scientist's 'philosophy of guided weapons' might lead him to propose certain kinds of 'objective research'). A 'progressive' job means one with possibilities of promotion.

8 Almost all college High Tables contain Fellows in both scientific and non-scientific subjects.

9 He took the examination in 1905.

10 It is, however, true to say that the compact nature of the managerial layers of English society—the fact that 'everyone knows everyone else'—means that scientists and non-scientists do in fact know each other as people more easily than in most countries. It is also true that a good many leading politicians and administrators keep up lively intellectual and artistic interests to a much greater extent, so far as I can judge, than is the case in the U.S. These are both among our assets.

11 I tried to compare American, Soviet and English education in 'New Minds for the New World', *New Statesman*, 6 September 1956.

12 The best, and almost the only, book on the subject.

13 It developed very fast. An English commission of inquiry into industrial productivity went over to the United States as early as 1865.

14 It is reasonable for intellectuals to prefer to live in the eighteenth-century streets of Stockholm rather than in Vallingby. I should myself. But it is not reasonable for them to obstruct other Vallingbys being built.

15 It is worth remembering that there must have been similar losses—spread over a much longer period—when men changed from the hunting and food gathering life to agriculture. For some, it must have been a genuine spiritual impoverishment.

16 This is not quite exact. In the states where higher education is most completely developed, for example, Wisconsin, about 95 per cent of children attend High School up to eighteen.

17 The U.S. is a complex and plural society, and the standards of colleges vary very much more than those of our universities. Some college standards are very high. Broadly, I think the generalisation is fair.

18 The number of engineers graduating per year in the United States is declining fairly sharply. I have not heard an adequate explanation for this.

19 The latest figures of graduates trained per year (scientists and engineers combined) are roughly U.K. 13,000, U.S.A. 65,000, U.S.S.R. 130,000.

20 One-third of Russian graduate engineers are women. It is one of our major follies that, whatever we say, we don't in reality regard women as suitable for scientific careers. We thus neatly divide our pool of potential talent by two.

21 It might repay investigation to examine precisely what education a hundred alpha plus creative persons in science this century have received. I have a feeling that a surprising proportion have not gone over the strictest orthodox hurdles, such as Part II Physics at Cambridge and the like.

22 The English temptation is to educate such men in sub-university institutions, which carry an inferior class-label. Nothing could be more ill-judged. One often meets American engineers who, in a narrow professional sense, are less rigorously trained than English products from technical colleges; but the Americans have the confidence, both social and individual, that is helped through having mixed with their equals at universities.

23 I have confined myself to the University population. The kind and number of technicians is another and a very interesting problem.

24 The concentration of our population makes us, of course, more vulnerable also in military terms.

25 There is one curious result in all major industrialised societies. The amount of talent one requires for the primary tasks is greater than any country can comfortably produce, and this will become increasingly obvious. The consequence is that there are no people left, clever, competent and resigned to a humble job, to keep the wheels of social amenities going smoothly round. Postal services, railway services, are likely slowly to deteriorate just because the people who once ran them are now being educated for different things. This is already clear in the United States, and is becoming clear in England.

26 In the United States the Lecture was published in hard covers (Cambridge University Press, 1959).

27 *Encounter*, May 1959, and subsequent issues.

28 J. Bronowski, *The Educated Man in 1984*. (Closing address to the Education Section of the British Association, 1955.)

29 Merle Kling, *New Republic*, 8 April 1957.

30 *New Statesman*, 6 October 1956.

31 *Sunday Times*, 10 and 17 March 1957.

32 I am referring to F. R. Leavis's *Two Cultures? The Significance of C. P. Snow* (first published, *Spectator*, 9 March 1962; republished in hard covers by Chatto and Windus in October 1962).

33 Leavis, *op. cit.*

34 *Spectator*, 23 March 1962 and later issues: other examples occur in the subsequent literature.

35 *Mit der Dummheit kämpfen Götter selbst vergebens.*

36 S. T. Coleridge, *On the Constitution of Church and State*, chapter v.

37 It is an interesting reflex of the British situation that the Royal Society, early this century, deliberately excluded from its scope the social sciences and other fields of learning which, in other countries, would be regarded as part of 'science' in its universal sense.

38 Cf. *The Search* (1934).

39 Good judges of the academic world, both American and English, sometimes tell me that I over-estimate American higher education.

40 Cf. Kenneth Richmond's *Culture and General Knowledge* (Methuen, 1963).

41 Alfred Kazin, *Contemporaries*, pp. 171–8 (Secker & Warburg, 1963).

42 That is, of course, judged by the standards of all human beings born up to the present time.

43 Cf. publications of I.N.E.D. (Institut National d'Etudes Démographiques), Paris. See, for example, M. Fleury and L. Henry, *Des registres paroissiaux à l'histoire de la population* (I.N.E.D., 1956); J. Meuvret, *Les crises de subsistances et la démographique de la France d'Ancien Régime. Population* (1946).

44 I.e. the peasants starved, and a small richer stratum survived. Recent research on seventeenth-century Sweden has shown that a year of semi-starvation was often followed by a year of epidemics which finished off the young, the old, and the debilitated.

45 E.g. P. Laslett and J. Harrison, 'Clayworth and Cogenhoe', in *Historical Essays 1600–1750* (A. & C. Black, 1963).

46 D. H. Lawrence, *Studies in Classic American Literature*, chapter 9.

47 The pseudo-scientific jargon keeps cropping up through the entire passage.

48 *The Rainbow*, chapter 12, provides one example out of many. 'Hatred sprang up in Ursula's heart. If she could she would smash the machine. Her soul's action should be the smashing of the great machine. If she could destroy the colliery, and make all the men of Wiggiston out of work, she would do it. Let them starve and grub in the earth for roots, rather than serve such a Moloch as this.'

This is an explicit statement of Luddite convictions: note the use of 'them'. It is *those others* who are exhorted to undergo the sacrifice and pay the price. But if Dostoevsky had been recommending Luddite activites, he wouldn't have stopped at random exhortation: he would have written out a programme by which the machines could be wrecked.

49 W. H. Auden (incidentally one of the few poets for a hundred years with both a scientific education and scientific insight) put it better in *In Memory of Yeats*.

50 In both the English and the American senses of the word.

51 There was an outburst of modernist literature (and other art) in Russia from the death of Chekhov (1904) until the Revolution and slightly after. When contemporary Russians say, as they sometimes do, that they have been through all that and don't think much of it, they are not inventing their case.

52 Dame Edith Sitwell, on being asked whether she was to be included among modernists or not, replied that whichever way was chosen she would consider it wrong.

53 *Partisan Review Anthology*, *1962*. I might mention that I was perplexed by Trilling's essay about *The Two*

Cultures (*Commentary*, June 1959). Nothing is more tedious than a writer claiming he is being misrepresented. It is usually his own fault. But I felt like saying that Trilling was attributing to me views on literature which I haven't expressed and don't hold: and attacking them by expressing views which, in the light of what he has written before and since, he doesn't appear to hold either. Martin Green has taken up the argument, more adequately, eloquently and dispassionately than I could have done: see *Essays in Criticism*, Winter 1963.

54 Stephen Spender, *The Struggle of the Modern* (Hamish Hamilton, 1962).

55 Georg Lukács, *The Meaning of Contemporary Realism* (Merlin Press, 1962—originally published in German in 1957).

56 Harry Levin, *The Gates of Horn* (Oxford, 1963)

57 I examined this problem in *Science and Government* and in the Appendix (published together, New American Library, 1962).